Door Busters

A ten lesson Bible study

breaking through doors that hold you back

Kathy A. Weckwerth

Door Busters
by Kathy A. Weckwerth
Best Life Ministries
P.O. Box 73
Benson, Minnesota 56215

Unless otherwise noted, all Scripture quotations
are taken from the following sources:
The New International Version of the Bible (NIV)
© 1984 by the International Bible Society.
Used by permission of Zondervan Bible Publishers.
The Message Copyright © by Eugene H. Peterson 1993, 1994,
1995, 1996, 2000, 2001, 2002. Used by permission of NavPress
Publishing Group.

Cover Design: Peter Grossman
Book Layout: Marea Anderson Designs
Editor: Susan C. Snow

Visit the author's website at www.KathyWeckwerth.com
Visit the author's ministry website at www.bestlifeministries.com

ISBN: 978-0-359-66049-0

To my three girls, Alexis, Chandra and Jenessa, who walked with me to face the doors. With God's help—we busted through. I continually thank Him for our freedom.

Door Busters

breaking through doors that hold you back

Lesson One

Your Door: The Unknown

"Never be afraid to trust an unknown future to a known God."

Corrie Ten Boom

Psalm 32:8 *"I will instruct you and teach you in the way you should go; I will counsel you with My eye upon you."*

Doors are a funny thing. They keep us in, they keep us out. Sometimes we find that concept frustrating, and sometimes we find that very same concept comforting. But, often in life whatever is on the other side of the door is where we know we should be.

We find ourselves walking up to that door, turning the knob and pushing our way through to the next place. Sometimes we'd like to push gently, and sometimes the door is so strong that we know we must *bust* our way through the doorway and take the resolute step into the next place in time and life.

The next place is always filled with one certainty ... *the unknown*. You will choose to *bust* through the stuck door and step over the threshold, but it always means you're in a different room, a different place, and different surroundings. With those surroundings comes the inevitable ... *change*.

But how do we face the doors in life and not run from the unknown? How do we push past the fear and have faith to *bust* through those doors that God is leading us to go through?

In Scripture we find many instances throughout history where someone faced a door that needed to be pushed hard, opened and walked through. Because doors keep us in or keep us out, there were times when those doors of impossibilities and insurmountable challenges gave someone the need to bust through to the other side.

This created many exceptional examples of unlikely door busters. Those who could have chosen to stay right where they were, did not because God pressed into their souls to move through a doorway. When that doorway was blocked, they ended up *busting* through it.

I am someone who loves to tour old homes and mansions. As a matter of fact, once inside the old homes, I like to dream and pretend that I reside there. I even like to pick out certain rooms as I'm touring, and tell myself that room would be a perfect place to read, or write, or practice piano.

One tour was through a stately old mansion located in a large Pennsylvania city. The front door was mammoth and heavy as I used my muscles to push it open. The tour guide was young and chatty, and repeatedly reminded us not to touch anything, brush up against anything, or ask too many questions.

We walked down a long, dark corridor that led to several huge bedrooms. Just as we got to the end of the massive hallway, I asked a question. I asked about something I saw behind a short bookcase and a small settee. There it was ... a glorious old carved door with a lovely glass knob.

"What's behind that door?" I questioned.

She snipped back an answer, "We're not allowed to go in there," and directed the group to continue down the hall.

I stayed back behind the others and gently grabbed the door knob. At first, I thought it was locked because it didn't budge. I gave one brief glance around me, pushed again and there it was! The door opened to a gorgeous old room, plainly decorated with simple features that included a small desk, standing lamp, an old pair of boots and a woman's hat on the desk. Pen, paper and books were peppered throughout the room. A tall window was covered with heavy dark draperies gently flapping back and forth as a crisp breeze whipped the papers to and fro.

That door had a purpose. The room behind it had a purpose. I was going to make sure I busted through the obstacles to get to where I could see what it was all about.

That's what door busting means. We see a door, we know God is calling us to it, but there are obstacles in the way. Whatever it is that's behind that stuck door is where we need to be.

Maybe the door is stuck because the obstacles are placed as challenges that we must work through to grow our faith. Maybe the door is stuck because the enemy is trying to keep us from God's will. Or maybe the obstacles are things that we have placed in front of the door ourselves.

Perhaps there are small obstacles like someone telling you not to go there or do that. Perhaps there are large obstacles, like the big pieces of furniture that were in the way of the door to the secret room. They are the obstacles of opposition, challenges, health issues or financial troubles. You seek God, you feel His prompting. You just need to push a little harder to get to where you need to be, to where you belong.

Nevertheless, once a door has been busted open, you are faced with those lurking unknown details that hide in the corners of the room. You're faced with the hidden trials that are tucked neatly away in the closet, the dark angst lying under the rug, the quiet loneliness lurking behind the closed draperies, all quietly in place to create fear. It's all new and it's all different. Welcome to the unknown.

As I think about facing doors and busting them down, my mind takes me back to a time that I became a door buster.

It was late summer when I walked the lonely and difficult path of divorce. My ex-spouse had been involved with drugs and had been abusive to our children and me. A police raid would shut down the drug lab he and his friend ran. Consequently, I took my children and left the familiar rooms that were filled with pain and suffering.

One thing I knew for certain, God called me to a door and asked me to walk through it. But the doorway seemed blocked. I had no money, no direction, no home, and no confidence. It was as though those specific obstacles were strewn about the corridor of my life and blocked the glorious door of freedom that sported a glass knob of hope.

I questioned myself and God. If there was a door there, a door of freedom, wouldn't there be an easier way to walk through it?

After weeks of seeking God, I found Him. A new job opened in a neighboring community. The church that hired me not only offered me a new job, but they also offered us help in finding a new home.

The doors that were holding us back, were getting a great big shove. Although they were squeaky, they were opening. I was breaking through. The fear of the unknown, of whatever was behind the door, would sneak in and taunt me; but I was too tired and busy to listen.

I remember that muggy summer afternoon when I pulled my old Dodge into the driveway of the little 1950's home the church helped me secure. All alone, I pulled the key from my purse and determined to push past any obstacles that blocked the door. I knew how important it was to start over and try to put back the pieces of my broken life.

The screen door to the back porch made an eerie screeching sound as it opened, but I was not afraid. The key fit into the lock and I turned the knob. The door wouldn't budge. It seemed swollen from the hot, muggy weather, so I began to push harder. Shoulder to the door, one hefty shove and the door swung wide open. I felt strong and, for a moment, confidence crept back into my soul.

Once inside, I was faced with the unknown. As sweet and comforting as the little grandma-house was, I didn't know anything about owning a house, caring for a house, or living alone without my husband in a house.

As I began to open doors and closets that were new to me, I realized some truths about the unknown. I could face it with fear and trepidation which seemed very reasonable. I could face it with an overwhelming dread which seemed sensible. Or I could just bust through the door of my emotions and with God's help, I could figure it out. That one seemed logical and became my best choice.

I remember slowly walking upstairs, bare feet against the 1970's green shag carpeting, and pulling open an old closet door. Behind the door was a lovely warm aroma of cedar chips. Once the lights were turned on, I discovered a beautiful closet to keep our winter woolens safe from dreaded moths. The unknown was providing good things, neatly lined up next to the scary ones.

Tugging open a timeworn cabinet, I found a little stack of Bible verses written out in a grandma's handwriting. Words jumped off the page and brought comfort and healing, all the while they seared strength into my spirit.

In the garage, I found leftover tidbits of engine parts, a yardstick, broken lawn mower blades, and a beautiful abandoned 1940's rug. What was once unknown was being revealed.

The girls and I managed to keep things going without a snag until the winter. I faced the door of winter's unknowns. Nights of crying and regret, mornings of frozen water pipes, long days of shoveling snow, changing outdoor lights that were out of reach and paying for bills without child support.

Those unknowns became familiar and then became well-knowns. With each challenge, I learned to cry out to God. I placed my trust in Him. He helped me break down the doors of abuse and placed me on a new path through a busted down door of freedom.

The unknowns were no longer unknown, and the fears were faced one by one. The wonderful truth that life offers about fear is this: once we have courage to face the fear, the fear loses its power.

I learned to cope and deal with what was behind the door. But if I had never faced the door, braced myself, and reached out to push, shove and bust it down, we wouldn't have been let out of the prison we had been held in for so long.

> The wonderful truth that life offers about fear is this: once we have courage to face the fear, the fear loses its power.
>
>

Wouldn't it have been so much easier to know what was behind the door? Perhaps, but God uses those closed doors that seem stuck to build our relationship with Him. Will we trust Him? Will we face the doors with courage or will we walk away in fear? Will we stand before the doors and grab the knob to turn them and bust them open, or will we turn and run?

THREE THINGS YOU SHOULD KNOW ABOUT DOORS:

1. **God creates and allows doors** in our lives to give us opportunities to grow, and to make us more faith-filled.

2. **God is with us** as we face the doors. We are never alone.

3. **God wants you to be motivated** to seek Him and His answers for the doors, whether you are afraid, or ready to bust through.

Each day that you wake up, you are faced with doors of decisions. The average person makes 35,000 decisions a day. According to Cornell University, each of us makes an average of 226.7 decisions relating to food alone.

Decisions are placed in front of us continually. What will I wear? Should I take time to respond to these emails? Should I let my child be in soccer and cub scouts? Should I take the job? Should I wash the car? Should I get a dog?

We will use our decision-making skill to determine whether we want to open a door of opportunity or allow the door to remain closed. We will decide whether it's easy to open and walk through, or difficult. We will act on our decision by pushing through that door, breaking it down if it opens with difficulty, or if we'll simply walk away.

Perhaps we'll feel like we don't have what it takes to face all the unknowns behind the door. Perhaps they will seem too difficult, too big, and are too much work. Maybe we'll feel like busting through that door is simply impossible.

Chuck Swindoll says, *"The best framework for the Lord God to do His most ideal work is when things are absolutely impossible and we feel totally unqualified to handle it. That's His favorite circumstance. Those*

7

are His ideal working conditions."

When we're facing the doors, God knows that if we're listening to His direction, we'll approach those doors and if they need a little shove, with His help, we'll bust through them. We just need to determine that we're willing to make the decision to move ahead, even if it's into the unknown.

The Bible is filled with incredible stories of simple average people doing complex, out-of-the-box antics, all because they were willing. Not necessarily able ... but willing! God looks for those who are everyday-ordinaries to work through, because in those ordinary lives, the willing are blessed and God is glorified.

In the Gospel of Luke, there is a story of a selfish sinner named Zacchaeus. Zacchaeus was determined to bust through a door that had huge obstacles set in front of it. An everyday-ordinary. A scoundrel. Disliked and disowned. Yet the Savior is calling him to a door.

Scripture tells us Zacchaeus was *"a son of Abraham,"* which meant he was a true Jew, from the lineage of Abraham himself. Jesus knew this about him, and we're reminded what the Father God calls Himself in Exodus 3:6 to Moses, *"I am the God of thy father, the God of Abraham, the God of Isaac, and the God of Jacob ..."*

Look Up: Genesis 22:17a

"I will surely bless you (Abraham) *and make your descendants as numerous as the stars in the sky and as the sand on the seashore."*

Jesus was traveling to Jerusalem and came to the town of Jericho, not quite twenty miles from Jerusalem. Jericho was a strategic crossroads for those in ancient Palestine. Located about forty-two miles from the Jordan River, the city was one of the main paths across the Judean desert. The city of Jericho was known for its crops of fruits, vegetables and balsam. The region was prosperous at the time this story took place.

In the Jewish tradition, they abhorred tax collectors. Scripture tells us that Zacchaeus served as a chief tax collector who had other officers serving underneath him.

Look Up: Luke 19:2

"A man was there by the name of Zacchaeus; he was a chief tax collector and was wealthy."

Unlike the meaning of Zacchaeus' name, "pure or innocent", this tax collector held neither of those attributes. Tax collectors were typically greedy and disliked by the Jews because they collaborated with the Roman government to charge the people with excessive taxes.

The tax collectors would gather the tax money for the government, charging extra, and would skim off the top, pocketing the extra for themselves. Zacchaeus was no different.

Archaeology digs have uncovered that the city of Jericho was the location where King Herod the Great built many impressive buildings at a great cost to the public. This would probably demonstrate to us what kind of a city it was, where taxes were high, and greed was rampant.

Unpopular with the crowds, Zacchaeus moved in to see Jesus on that day, but he was limited by his own human shortcomings. The furniture was stacked in front of the door of opportunity. Scripture says Zacchaeus was short in stature.

Look Up: Luke 19:3

"He wanted to see who Jesus was, but because he was short he could not see over the crowd."

Zacchaeus was disliked, and his sins were well-known throughout the entire community. The hindrances were all around him and the door of opportunity lay directly in front of him. He was called to see the Savior, but he couldn't quite get the door open. There was stuff everywhere. Push as hard as he might, he was limited, *but God was not.*

The idea came to Zacchaeus to climb a tree. If he could just catch a glimpse of this man named Jesus, perhaps he could understand who was healing the sick, the blind and the lame, and was teaching about the Kingdom of God.

The obstacle for him was that the door that was stuck. The desire and the will were there to bust it down. Find a way. Make a way. Climb the tree. Zacchaeus did just that and from the tree he was able to see Jesus. But he's faced with the unknown. Who was this man they said was the Son of God? Who was this man who was known as the Savior? What would happen after he pushed his way through the door of opportunity?

Look Up: Luke 19:4-10
"So he ran ahead and climbed a sycamore-fig tree to see him, since Jesus was coming that way.

"When Jesus reached the spot, He looked up and said to him, 'Zacchaeus, come down immediately. I must stay at your house today.' So he came down at once and welcomed him gladly.

"All the people saw this and began to mutter, 'He has gone to be the guest of a sinner.'

"But Zacchaeus stood up and said to the Lord, 'Look, Lord! Here and now I give half of my possessions to the poor, and if I have cheated anybody out of anything, I will pay back four times the amount.'

"Jesus said to him, 'Today salvation has come to this house, because this

man, too, is a son of Abraham. For the Son of Man came to seek and to save the lost.'"

Jesus used His favorite title for Himself in verse 10, when He called Himself, *"Son of Man."* That title was used 81 times within the Gospels by Jesus Himself. The name "Son of Man" can be found in the book of Daniel, as Daniel recited what he would see in the future. In Daniel 7:13, he said, *"there before me was one like a Son of Man,"* and he continued to say that this Son of Man would one day establish an everlasting kingdom. Jesus was letting those around Him know who He was, with a reminder of what the future held for those who believe in Him as Savior.

In those moments, on that dry, dusty road, with crowds of onlookers and a tax-collecting-sinner who was seeking the Savior, Scripture shows us what happened to Zacchaeus. Jesus spotted him in the sycamore tree *(a sturdy tree, 30-40 feet high, with a short trunk and wide lateral branches capable of holding a grown man)* and told him to come down from the tree so he could go to Zacchaeus' home.

He called Zacchaeus to a door of opportunity. Bust down the door, change your ways, change your life.

Jesus has no limits. No doors are in His way. The door that has been broken through has unknown blessings and rewards, because Zacchaeus made a choice, a determined decision to seek after Christ, with no doors holding him back.

Matthew Henry states in his commentary, *"Those who sincerely desire a sight of Christ, like Zacchaeus, will break through opposition, and take pains to see him."*

Breaking down the doors that hold us back gives us the direct blessing of receiving what God has in store for us. Freedom, new life, hope, a changed heart, the newness of God ... all the things that partner with the unknown if we but break through the boundaries.

Look Up: Isaiah 43:19

"See, I am doing a new thing! Now it springs up; do you not perceive it? I am making a way in the wilderness and streams in the wasteland."

Life for Zacchaeus would never be the same. The same Savior who healed the sick, made the lame to walk, spoke with adulterers and unbelievers, made His way to a sinner known by all ... the tax collector. And there the Savior stopped to say ... You chose me ... friend, I chose you.

No longer did greed corrupt his heart. Zacchaeus had broken through the sin and condemnation that were blocking doors to a new life, and he offered to pay back those whom he had cheated.

Why did he say he would pay back four times the amount? The Roman law required this when someone was cheated. The Jewish penalty of restitution for stealing was set up for them in Exodus.

Look Up: Exodus 22:1

"Whoever steals an ox or a sheep and slaughters it or sells it must pay back five head of cattle for the ox and four sheep for the sheep."

The same small man who oppressed the Jews and held them back, broke down doors of physical limitations, oppression, judgment, pride and sin, was released into freedom.

Breaking down a door to get to Jesus meant that God showed up. Jesus could have had supper at anyone's home, but He chose the sinner who had broken down barriers to get to Him.

FIVE STEPS WHEN FACING AN UNKNOWN DOOR:

STEP ONE: What does scripture say?

Proverbs 2:6, *"For the Lord gives wisdom; from His mouth comes knowledge and understanding."*

Proverbs 3:5-6, *"Trust in the Lord with all of your heart and do not lean on your own understanding. In all your ways acknowledge Him, and He will make your paths straight."*

Whenever we need help, we go to God. Where do we find Him? Through His Spirit and through His Word. God's Word is filled with answers. My daddy used to hold out his hands and say, "Kathleen, in this hand are all of life's problems, and in this hand is Scripture with all of life's answers."

STEP TWO: What are the facts?

Proverbs 18:13, *"He who gives an answer before he hears, it is folly and shame to him."*

Proverbs 18:17, *"The first to plead his case seems right, until another comes and examines him."*

Write the facts down on a paper so you can see them. What is truth? What do you know about the door? Why is it there? What might it provide? How will it affect you and your family? What could it do to further God's good work in your life and for His Kingdom? Is it one you're going to have to ask God for help to bust down?

STEP THREE: What is my emotional state?

Proverbs 19:2, *"Also it is not good for a person to be without knowledge, and he who makes haste with his feet errors."*

Proverbs 21:5, *"The plans of the diligent lead surely to advantage, but everyone who is hasty comes surely to poverty."*

Are you in a place where you are overwhelmed with obstacles like Zacchaeus? Have you been taken over by limitations and the unknown, and you can't face the door? Do you want to go back and forget there's a door of opportunity?

Complacency is a bad word in God's Kingdom. Turning around and wishing that something wasn't there, when in fact God is using the door as a learning lesson and an opportunity, is refusing to allow God's hand to move in your life. Sitting back and doing nothing doesn't work with God.

STEP FOUR: What is my motivation?

Proverbs 16:2, *"All the ways of a man are clean in his own sight, but the Lord weighs the motives."*

Proverbs 20:9, *"Who can say, 'I have cleansed my heart, I am pure from my sin?'"*

Are you opening a door that will serve just you and harm others? Is it a door of opportunity that is solely based on wealth or notoriety? Or is it something God will use for His glory?

STEP FIVE: What are my trusted friends and family saying?

Proverbs 11:14, *"Where there is no guidance the people fall, but in an abundance of counselors there is victory."*

Proverbs 18:1-2, *"He who separates himself seeks his own desire. He quarrels against all sound wisdom. Fools find no pleasure in understanding but delight in airing their own opinions."*

Seeking others and their opinions is Biblical. When we need help determining if busting through a door is God's will, we can seek God, read His Word and ask our friends and wise counsel for their thoughts.

Let's look at Zacchaeus using those five helpful steps:

STEP ONE: What does scripture say?
Zacchaeus is doing anything he can to get to see Christ.

STEP TWO: What are the facts?
He knows he is a sinner and a cheat, and he is unpopular with the crowd. He is too short to see Jesus over them.

STEP THREE: What is my emotional state?
He is overwhelmed but determined to bust through the door of opportunity to face the unknown.

STEP FOUR: What is my motivation?
To see Jesus, the One whom others have said is the true awaited Messiah.

STEP FIVE: What are my trusted friends and family saying?
Without reading about any specific friends, we know the crowd is questioning why Jesus would ever go to this sinner's home.

God is always about creating opportunities for growth. When Jesus gave Zacchaeus a chance, it propelled him into repentance and a changed life. That's the unknown behind the door. Great things for Zacchaeus.

The doors in life affect us. The doors in life affect others. Busting down doors can change our lives and the lives of others. Jesus Christ is truly the only One who can open and shut doors, but if He has determined that He wants to offer us an opportunity, it won't matter if there are obstacles. Jesus will make sure that He is there with a strong shoulder and the right key to help us push past and get through.

Look Up: Revelation 3:7

"These are the words of Him who is holy and true, who holds the key of David. What He opens no one can shut, and what He shuts no one can open."

I have found in this life that every door that has been placed before me was a faith-builder, a mind-stretcher, and a life-changer. That's how your door can be if you choose Christ. Push a little bit and determine that you need to bust through whatever it is that's blocking it. Don't fear the unknown because God is with you.

We are never alone. God helps us to face the doors. He will provide the courage and the knowledge to open them, break them down, and bust through them. And when we seek Him and obey Him, He'll come through with blessings untold.

My corridor was abuse. My door was blocked with obstacles of fear. My unknown was light, life and freedom.

Get busting down your own doors ... freedom's calling you.

Questions:

1. Have you ever faced a door of opportunity and felt afraid to walk through it because of the unknowns? If so, did you push past your fears or did you walk away?

2. Have you ever felt obstacles in the way of your opportunities and become discouraged by them? How did you respond to those obstacles? Were they self-created or real?

3. How strong is your desire to spend time with the Savior? Are you regularly seeking God in Scripture and prayer? Are you listening for His inner promptings and direction for your life? If not, what can you do this week to make a cognitive change?

4. Right now, God is working in your life to help you overcome fear and doubt. What emotions are you struggling with as you read this chapter? How will you move forward and bust open the door of opportunity?

Look Up:

1. Joshua 1:9

2. Psalm 23:4

3. Psalm 34:4

4. Psalm 94:19

5. Isaiah 43:1

6. Matthew 6:34

7. John 14:27

Songs:

Hymn ~ *"Great Is Thy Faithfulness"* (Thomas Obadiah Chisholm)

Contemporary ~ *"Good, Good Father"* (Chris Tomlin)

Closing Prayer:

Dear Jesus,

You call me to great opportunities.

Help me to trust You to remove obstacles
and have faith that all the unknowns
will be revealed in Your perfect timing.

Help me be ready to open doors.

In Jesus' Name, *Amen.*

Door Busters

Lesson Two

Leah's Door: Rejection

"Successful people reject rejection."

John Maxwell

Door Busted: In the last lesson, when we studied the door of the unknown, we learned that God creates and allows opportunities in our lives for us to grow and mature. These opportunities can be unknown when they're presented to us as a door. Often that door seems impossible to open because the obstacle in front of it is our fear of that *unknown*. God wants us to trust Him to bust through and experience life to its fullest!

Isaiah 53:3, *"He was despised and rejected by men, a man of sorrows and acquainted with grief. And we hid, as it were, our faces from Him; He was despised, and we did not esteem Him."*

There are times in life when God calls us to doors of change. It's an adventure, something new, something exciting. But often in life, the doors He calls us to will have obstacles in the way. They will have challenges that make the door hard to open. We can be assured that the door is God's will because of inner promptings from the Holy Spirit, God's Word leading us, others' advice, and details falling into place.

But what do we do about the obstacles?

One of the challenges that can stand in front of a door of opportunity can be *rejection*. We might feel God calling us, see things working out, but people around us are rejecting the idea of the door. Or perhaps, you believe you're supposed to do something, but the people who have the

21

deciding power have rejected you. How do you proceed and bust down the door?

When you look at the word *rejection*, it evokes the same emotions in every human being. Emotions of grief, sadness, a questioning spirit, and hopelessness flood the soul. All are generated by simple acts of rejection.

Rejection can steal energy, break wills and squash out life. It can lead people into misery, anger and doubt. To be rejected is painful. To reject others is often dismissed by our own self-convinced conscience. But when it comes to God and His doors, rejection is most frequently used to propel someone to something bigger and greater in life. God uses rejection to teach lessons, produce faith and grow maturity.

Webster's Dictionary states that *to* **reject** something means, *"to refuse to accept or agree in something because it is not good enough or not the right thing, to be unkind to somebody, something or somebody not wanted."*

Everything about the description makes me cringe. I've dealt with rejection often throughout my life, as I'm sure you have as well. I have been rejected by others. I have rejected others. I have been rejected for employment, rejected in love, rejected in friendship, and rejected by church people. There have been moments in this life where I have felt rejected by God.

But here's the thing I know about rejection ... Jesus discovered a way to deal with rejection. He dealt with it when the Scribes, Pharisees, His family and even the Roman government officials rejected Him.

If we don't learn how to deal with rejection, it will bury itself in our souls and will wheedle its way into how we think and act. It will move into the home of our hearts and begin to grow into depression, resentment, anger and bitterness.

More than anything, I want us to **know** that Jesus understands. He gets what it means to be rejected. More than any human being on earth from the beginning of time up until now, Jesus understands rejection.

Rejection can get in the way of the doors that God calls us to open. Because it is so incredibly painful, we tend to look the other way if rejection is nearby.

Isaiah 53:3 in *The New Century Version Bible* states it this way: *"He was hated and rejected by people. He had much pain and suffering. People would not even look at him. He was hated, and we didn't even notice him."*

Have you ever experienced rejection where you were hated? Where someone wouldn't even look at you? I have. The feelings you experienced include a deep hurt and a panicked state of shock. You may experience an enormous desire to change whoever is delivering the rejection. You think ... accept me, like me, care about me. But rejection means this won't happen. How do we deal with rejection?

Following a leisurely route, I traveled from my elderly mother's home in southwest Iowa back to my home in Minnesota. Winding roads that were bent around fields of grain and small ponds made the trip incredibly peaceful and relaxing. Until I received a call from my husband, Farmer Dean.

"Ma'am," he questioned, "did you change the password on our computer?"

"No, what are you talking about?" I asked.

"Well, the computer won't let me in. I keep trying to enter the password, but it keeps rejecting it. I don't know what to do," Dean stated anxiously.

I convinced him to stop working on the problem and walk away from the computer. But something deep inside of me began to feel desperate, and I wondered how we would combat the rejection.

When I arrived home, I was confident that my computer would know me. After all, it was me! I worked on it day and night. It knew me, and it had never rejected me before.

I shut everything down, rebooted the computer, and there it was, the place to put in my password. It happened just as the farmer said it would. I was rejected. I was hurt, shocked and wanted to change the mind of ... *my computer!*

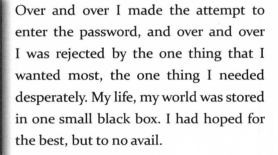

I learned that God, our Creator, has the power and authority to override any rejection that comes against us!

Over and over I made the attempt to enter the password, and over and over I was rejected by the one thing that I wanted most, the one thing I needed desperately. My life, my world was stored in one small black box. I had hoped for the best, but to no avail.

The next day, Farmer Dean and I took a vacation day together and drove to a nearby city to visit the computer nerds at the Best Buy store. The man standing behind the counter, dressed in black pants, white shirt and a black tie, with glasses falling off his nose stated kindly, "No worries, Ma'am. We have the *power* and the *authority* to *override the rejection.*"

We were shocked. How was that possible? We watched. With a small black jump drive inserted into our computer, they did it. My life was recovered and rejection was overcome.

From that moment on, I safeguarded myself. I learned to face any and all opportunities God gave me where rejection was lurking. I learned that God, our Creator, has the power and authority to override any rejection that comes against us!

I went home and studied about backing up my work on an external jump drive. I found a strategy on how to deal with rejection, so it would not take me down and take me out! I was ready to face new doors of opportunity!

I believe there are many reasons why people reject us. I believe they can reject our ideas, our actions, our attitudes, our looks, our ethnicity, our accent, our faith. Rejection is thrown at us for all kinds of reasons.

Some reasons are as follows: jealousy, control, competition, no connection with us, not their taste, style or opinion. Sometimes we create a trigger that reminds them of hurt or pain in their own current circumstances or their past.

REJECTION MAY OCCUR IN A VARIETY OF CIRCUMSTANCES:

EXAMPLE ONE: A young woman meets a gregarious teacher at an event and really likes him, but he's not attracted to her. Instead, he's attracted to Sherry Sunshine. Immediately the rejected young woman discards the sweet conversation Sherry tries to make with her because she's jealous that Sherry is accepted, and she is not. *Rejection.*

EXAMPLE TWO: A man at work named Harvey doesn't like the fact that things are changing at his company. He likes things the way they used to be. Harvey is at a board meeting when his co-workers recommend a great idea. Out of a spirit of competition and control, Harvey rejects their idea. *Rejection.*

EXAMPLE THREE: A kind, attractive man asks a divorced mother of three out on a date. Over a one-year time frame, they casually go out on dates, chat on the phone, and develop a friendship. The woman feels a strong connection and falls in love. The man calls her up one day, cancels their date and says, "Sorry, you just don't do it for me. I can't see you anymore." *Rejection.*

EXAMPLE FOUR: A young mother can no longer help with her church youth group because a teen has been coming to the church with bruises on her arms and legs. Instead of being kind to the teen, she rejects her. The situation reminds her too much of the anger she experiences in her home and hides her hurt from everyone. *Rejection.*

Each of these examples describe various instances of rejection. Rejection isn't just one simple example. Rejection is complex.

What does Scripture teach us about how to deal with doors that have the spirit of rejection lurking in front of them?

Many great characters of the Bible faced rejection. People rejected Jeremiah when he told them to change or God would impose His wrath. Jesus was rejected all the way to the cross. The women at Jesus' tomb were rejected when they told the disciples Jesus had risen again and was alive. And Stephen was rejected when he witnessed to others about the Messiah.

There is one story in scripture that stands out the most about a door blocked with rejection. Two sisters teach about the hurt and pain of rejection. This story was perhaps the most difficult for me to read, walk through, and absorb, for this rejection I could understand at a deep level.

The story is of a young woman named Leah, her sister, Rachel and their husband, Jacob.

Before we begin, I want to tell you that God loved Jacob. At times when we read this story, it's hard to understand that God would love someone who seemed so selfish and such a trickster in his prior years, but this example gives us hope. If God could love someone who was such a sinner in our opinion, how could He not love us?

God's love for Jacob was at a deep level because God refers to Himself in scripture as *"The God of Abraham, Isaac and Jacob."* God says this, or refers to Himself with this same title, in Exodus 3:6, 3:15, 6:3, 6:8, 33:1, and Leviticus 26:42, as well as in the books of Numbers, Deuteronomy, Kings and Jeremiah. Jacob was loved by God.

Today, as we study Scripture, we can see that other people have walked up to doors and have been met with rejection. We don't have to soak it in, we don't have to carry it with us, and we don't have to ruminate over those instances or people who have rejected us. Instead, we can learn to push past and bust down the door of rejection.

Please open your Bible to Genesis 29. At this point in the story, Jacob was fleeing from the wrath of his brother, Esau. Jacob headed north to the home of his mother's brother, Laban. Laban had two daughters, Leah, the oldest and her younger sister, Rachel.

As Jacob headed to the watering well in the field, he saw his cousin, a shepherdess named, Rachel. She's beautiful and it's love at first sight for Jacob. She ran to tell her daddy, Laban, that Jacob had arrived for a visit. Here we pick up the story in verse 14.

Look Up: Genesis 29:14-20
"Then Laban said to him, 'You are my own flesh and blood.' After Jacob had stayed with him for a whole month, Laban said to him, 'Just because you are a relative of mine, should you work for me for nothing? Tell me what your wages should be.'

"Now Laban had two daughters; the name of the older was Leah, which means cow—and the name of the younger was Rachel—which means lamb. Leah had weak eyes, but Rachel had a lovely figure and was beautiful. Jacob was in love with Rachel and said, 'I'll work for you seven years in return for your younger daughter Rachel.'"

Theologians say the description of Leah could have referred to a pale color of eyes, or bad eyesight. Some thought she was cross-eyed, and some said it meant she was unattractive.

"Laban said, 'It's better that I give her to you than to some other man. Stay here with me.' So Jacob served seven years to get Rachel, but they seemed like only a few days to him because of his love for her."

Listen to those words again ... *"but they seemed like only a few days to him because of his love for her."*

Friends, I've seen that kind of love before in my own mother and father. My daddy would talk about my mother, look at my mother, and value my mother like she was the only woman on Planet Earth. When I married Farmer Dean, I knew that this was the same kind of love I found for my own life.

This is a deep love. So passionate was Jacob about Rachel that he would work seven years (that's 2,555 days) to have her as his wife. Yet, he says it felt like only a few days because of how much he loved her. That's real love.

Look Up: Genesis 29:21-32
"Then Jacob said to Laban, 'Give me my wife. My time is completed, and I want to lie with her.'

*"So Laban brought together all the people of the place and gave a feast. But when evening came, he took his daughter **Leah** and brought*

her to Jacob, and Jacob lay with her. And Laban gave his servant Zilpah to his daughter as her attendant.

"When morning came, there was Leah! So Jacob said to Laban, 'What is this you have done to me? I served you for Rachel, didn't I? Why have you deceived me?'

"Laban replied, 'It is not our custom here to give the younger daughter in marriage before the older one. Finish this daughter's bridal week; then we will give you the younger one also, in return for another seven years of work.'

"And Jacob did so. He finished the week with Leah, and then Laban gave him his daughter Rachel to be his wife. Laban gave his servant Bilhah to his daughter Rachel as her attendant. **Jacob lay with Rachel also, and his love for Rachel was greater than his love for Leah.** And he worked for Laban another seven years.

"When the Lord saw that Leah was not loved, He enabled her to conceive, but Rachel remained childless. Leah became pregnant and gave birth to a son. She named him Reuben, for she said, **'It is because the Lord has seen my misery. Surely my husband will love me now.'**"

Reuben's name means: I AM SEEN.

What sad words when Leah said, *"Surely my husband will love me now."* What's wrong with that husband, Jacob! What was Leah thinking?

This was the manipulation of rejection. The enemy uses it to cast us down, make us believe we are no good, and emphasize that *we are less.* Sometimes that rejection is placed on us simply to hold us down.

Yet, Leah was trying to rise above it. She thought, "If I just do this one thing, my husband will love me." We've all done it … if I just do this one thing, my boss will give me that raise. If I just lose this much weight, he won't have an affair. If I just act nicer to her, she'll be my friend.

I know this role so well because I came from a broken marriage. My previous spouse was a liar, a drug abuser and a cheat. I tried to stand up to the rejection believing if I just did this or that ... it would change. It never did.

When I weighed 110 pounds I was still told I was fat. When I had been a participant in the Miss Southwest Iowa pageant, which leads to Miss USA, I was told I was ugly. I was a good B+ student and I was told I was stupid. Rejection tries to wheedle its way into your mind and soul and say *you are less.*

"Surely, my husband will love me now," Leah observed. The door that God was calling Leah to included acceptance of herself and her circumstances. She can't quite reach it. She loves, but she is not loved. She can't get to the door of freedom because the obstacle is rejection. All she could think about was who was around her. Her servant, her husband, her sister, all became her focus. She was an ugly-unlovable, or so she believed, because the rejection had taken over.

We've seen it before. Someone says I'm leaving you for another. You think if I just do this, it will stop them from leaving. Why do you want to stop them? If I just do this ... you'll do that. Is the acceptance so incredibly valuable that you stop short of opening the door, sell your soul, and shortchange your life to become something you are not, only for that one act of acceptance?

Look Up: Genesis 29:33
"She conceived again, and when she gave birth to a son she said, 'Because the Lord heard that I am not loved, He gave me this one too.' So she named him Simeon."

Simeon's name means: I AM HEARD.

Look Up: Genesis 29:34-35
*"Again she conceived, and when she gave birth to a son she said, 'Now at last my husband **will become attached to me**, because I have borne him three sons.' So he was named Levi."*

Levi's name means: I AM ATTACHED OR CONNECTED.

The door is there. An opportunity to feel differently about herself and life. Rejection blocks the door. Whatever Leah is trying, it's not going to measure up to the ooey-gooey love that Jacob feels for her sister, Rachel. Having babies isn't working. Look at what happened.

*"She conceived again, and when she gave birth to a son she said, '**This time I will praise the Lord.**' So she named him Judah. Then she stopped having children."*

Judah's name means: PRAISE.

She not only stopped having children for a while, but she finally got it. Leah had been looking for her self-worth ever since she got rejected the morning after the wedding night. She didn't understand it was right there behind the door of opportunity that God placed before her. An opportunity to change the way she felt about herself. To accept the most important love of all ... the love of God.

Leah didn't understand that rejection could simply be overridden by the authority and power of her Creator. Our worth can't be placed in the hands of humans. When we are looking for affirmation in places other than God, looking for our self-worth in what we do, how we look, what we can accomplish, we will place our lives in the hands of those who can reject us, and our footing will be offset. We'll fall!

Shannon L. Alder says, *"There will always be someone willing to hurt you, put you down, gossip about you, belittle your accomplishments and judge your soul. It is a fact that we all must face. However, if you realize that God is a best friend that stands beside you when others cast stones you will never be afraid, never feel worthless and never feel alone."*

I think back to many years ago at a large church in the Twin Cities. I was hired as their Director of Worship and Creative Arts. I arrived at work and felt confident that God was doing good things in me and through me. The attendance was growing, the team was growing, I was growing.

After about a month on the job, there was a knock on my door. There stood one of my team members, a feisty redhead with freckles and a mean attitude. She constantly rejected every single idea I had. All my recommendations were placed before the team. She rejected song suggestions, drama ideas, creative elements, dates, times, places, meetings and ME! Although she stretched my patience level, I remained prayerful, faithful, and optimistic that she would get on board.

The door opened to the redhead that day. She looked at me with hard, steely-gray eyes and said, "I reject you. I don't believe you, so I reject you."

I was puzzled and answered, "Huh?"

She responded, "No one could be this nice. I reject you."

She shut the door and walked away. I didn't know it at the time but found out later that she had struggled with rejection her entire childhood. Passed from foster home to foster home as a little girl, she was never completely loved. She let rejection stop her from every opportunity God placed in front of her. I pushed past the rejection even though it stung, and she eventually came around. Not everyone will. Some will reject and despise you no matter what you do or how patient you are.

In the story of Jacob, Rachel and Leah, Leah eventually had two more sons and a daughter named Dinah. That made six sons and a daughter for Leah. Leah's maidservant had two sons with Jacob as well. Rachel had Joseph and Benjamin. Rachel's maidservant also had two sons with Jacob. These sons are the twelve men who make up the twelve tribes of Israel.

The story turns about completely in Genesis 43, when on the way to Bethlehem, Rachel died giving birth to Benjamin. Jacob buried her on that trip. But at the end of Leah's life, the one whom he rejected, Leah, is buried in the family plot next to Jacob's family, Abraham, Sarah, Isaac and Rebekah. Something changed.

Rejection is a strange thing. Sometimes it can turn and twist about. Sometimes people reject an idea or a person, but in the end, they learn to embrace and love that idea or that person. Sometimes. But sometimes it doesn't work out.

THREE LESSONS TO LEARN FROM REJECTION:

We are going to look at three points that will help us focus and understand how to deal with doors that have rejection blocking their entrance.

LESSON ONE: Rejection is part of life.
You are going to be rejected. Humans will reject your ideas, your love, and your actions. Sometimes you can figure it out and sometimes you won't be able to make sense of the craziness.

Humans rejected the Son of God.

Look Up: I Peter 2:4

"As you come to Him, the living Stone—rejected by humans but chosen by God and precious to Him."

I've met people whose own mothers or fathers rejected them.

Look Up: John 1:11

"He came to that which was His own, but His own did not receive Him."

LESSON TWO: Rejection is painful.

Rejection stings. When we are not accepted, it hurts. It's human nature.

Look Up: John 15:18

"If the world hates you, keep in mind that it hated Me first."

LESSON THREE: Rejection has purpose.

God uses evil, trouble and sin to twist it into good in our lives. We're not alone.

Look Up: Luke 10:16

"Whoever listens to you listens to Me; whoever rejects you rejects Me; but whoever rejects Me rejects Him who sent Me."

When we get so focused on rejection, we don't remember the truth. When we get so focused on rejection, we don't look at what we have. We look around us and we forget to look up.

Look Up: Psalm 94:14

"For the Lord will not reject His people; He will never forsake His inheritance."

FOUR STEPS TO HANDLE REJECTION:

STEP ONE: Be objective and realistic.

If you receive rejection, realize that God has something else for you behind the door if you just push past.

STEP TWO: Be forgiving.

Let go of the rejection because anger and bitterness harden our souls. Resentment will change who you are and open a door for the enemy to come in.

STEP THREE: Be accepting.

Don't fight what God is doing. You might think it's the worst thing that's ever happened when people in your life reject you. That person who doesn't like you, that boss who doesn't see your potential, that person who you think should be your friend doesn't reciprocate—accept it and move forward. Bust down the door.

STEP FOUR: Be motivated.

When you feel rejected, use that rejection as motivation. Get motivated to find a different job, a different person to date, a different house to purchase, a different friend to make.

Life is filled with twists involving rejection. Many have seen the door of opportunity in life only to have rejection as an obstacle on their path.

- In the 1850s, a biologist determined that disease was spread by germs. He made the discovery after three of his five children died from infectious diseases. When he first put forward his theory, his ideas were rejected. Today, we are thankful for the discoveries that Louis Pasteur made.

- When a young Henry Ford tried to present his project of a motor to a group of industrialists, he was rejected. However, Thomas Edison continued to encourage him and today everybody is reaping the benefits of Ford's idea: affordable vehicles for an average citizen.

• And lastly, my favorite example. As a young child, Walter delivered papers every morning at 4:30 a.m. In 1918 he was rejected from the army for being too young. Fired for lacking creativity, Walter decided to create his own cartoon character, a little mouse named Mickey, but his idea was rejected 300 times.

Walt Disney became a billionaire, because he didn't let rejection take him down. Disney stated, *"All the adversity I've had in my life, all my troubles and obstacles, have strengthened me."*

In this world where we will be rejected, it's important to know that we are loved by God. When the world tries to insert the password of who they think we are, who they want us to become, there is One who has the key to override their authority. God's power, His authority in being the Author and Creator of our lives, is all that counts.

Leah looked at the obstacle of rejection and tried three times to change things. Finally, when she looked at God for her acceptance, it busted down the door! She received the blessing of Judah.

Leah looked for her self-worth from another human but was continually rejected. When Leah used God as her password, her life was recovered.

The door was busted down and we find out that God's plan behind the door was bigger than Leah could have imagined.

Our worth can't be placed in the hands of others. When we look for affirmation in places other than God, look for self-worth in what we do, how we look, or what we can accomplish, we place our lives in the hands of those who can reject us, and we will be hurt.

Give your life over to the One who has the power and authority to override rejection!

Look Up: Hebrews 7:14
"For it is clear that our Lord descended from the tribe of Judah ..."

Look Up: Revelation 5:5
"Then one of the elders said to me 'Do not weep! See the lion of the tribe of Judah, the Root of David, has triumphed. He is able to open the scroll and its seven seals.'"

From the rejection of Jacob comes Judah. From the lineage of Judah comes Jesus.

Some of the most beautiful things in life come out of rejection.

Leah's door was blocked with obstacles of rejection. Her unknown on the other side of the door was self-confidence, freedom, and acceptance of the love of God.

Face the challenge. Don't accept rejection as it tries to make its way into your heart. Push the door ... just a little bit harder. There it is ... love and acceptance.

Questions:

1. Scripture tells us that Jesus Christ came out of the lineage of Leah's son, Judah. Why is that significant to us regarding rejection and looking to others for acceptance?

2. Leah looked at others to formulate her happiness. Have you ever acted this way or are you doing this right now? Perhaps someone's rejection has made you angry and bitter. What did you learn from Leah about how to change your perspective?

3. Name a time when you or someone you know, manipulated someone who was blocking a door with rejection, hoping to get them to change their mind. How did it work out?

4. Which of the Four Steps to Handle Rejection resonates the most to you right now in your journey? What will you do this week to make a change and bust down a door?

Look Up:

1. Psalm 27:9-10

2. Psalm 34:17-20

3. Psalm 94:14

4. Isaiah 53:3

5. John 1:11

6. Romans 8:1

7. Romans 8:31

Songs:

Hymn ~ *"Blessed Assurance"* (Thomas Obadiah Chisholm)

Contemporary ~ *"King of My Heart"* (John Mark McMillan & Sarah McMillan)

Closing Prayer:

Dear Jesus,

I see a door of opportunity
in front of me.

Although I am excited
for Your plan,
I feel the scorn of rejection
in my path.

Help me look to You alone
for acceptance.

In Jesus' Name, *Amen.*

Lesson Three

Moses' Door: Attitude

*"Outlook determines outcome.
If we see only the problems, we will be defeated;
but if we see the possibilities in the problems,
we can have victory."*

Warren Wiersbe

Door Busted: In the last lesson, we learned from Leah that rejection is part of life and, although it is painful, it does have purpose. Scripture tells us that when we look for affirmation in places other than God, we will become hurt and disappointed. Our self-worth should come from the truth that God loves us, just as He created us.

John 14:23, *"Jesus replied, 'Anyone who loves me will obey my teaching. My Father will love them, and we will come to them and make our home with them.'"*

Do you ever struggle with your attitude? I mean really struggle with having a faith-filled attitude when everything through human eyes looks bleak. Are you a person with a glass half-empty and you see life as continually difficult? Or are you a person who sees the glass half-full and find yourself looking for a silver lining?

For years, I have balanced in the middle of a half-empty glass and a half-full one. It took me ages to understand how incredibly powerful my attitude was, not just to myself but to those whom I have influence over. Now, I make an effort to maintain a positive attitude. Now, I see God stretch my faith and show me His glory. Now, I know God works amidst

41

my life's simplest details.

When my daughter, Chandra was one year old, she had two little front teeth on the top of her mouth. When she smiled, everyone around her melted. Little blonde ringlets and sparkly, blue eyes made her simply adorable.

Chandra's only challenge was that while other babies her age were racing across the living room, she was still barely crawling. She had no desire to get up and walk, so I didn't push her.

One day, while I sorted through some boxes in the garage, I put Chandra in a baby walker and set her loose on the cement floor to scoot around. She was always a busy girl and I wasn't surprised when I heard a loud crash. But when I turned around, I was horrified! There was my baby, thrown from the walker onto the cement floor. She just missed a huge piece of sheet metal that had been leaning against the back door.

I couldn't decide which was scarier, the fact that her face could have been sliced up from the big piece of metal, or the fact that her mouth was bleeding profusely.

I'm one of those people who isn't good with blood. Chandra cried. I cried. Then I forced myself to look through the blood and see the source of the bleeding. An adorable little front tooth had been knocked out. I glanced around the floor, grabbed it, and headed inside.

I got Chandra quieted down and settled on the floor with her blanket. I stopped the bleeding and threw the tiny tooth in a bowl of ice water. After all, isn't that what people do when you sever a limb or finger?

I desperately grabbed the phone book and randomly dialed one dentist after the next without an answer. Sobbing, crying, shaking, I eventually reached a calm and kind dentist. Dr. Tom asked me to calm down, breathe deeply and slowly tell me what happened. He had been God-ordained for that moment in my life.

Dr. Tom gently asked, "Is your baby okay? Is anything else wrong? I'll wait right here while you check her entire head and body for any cuts, bruises or broken bones." I felt a slight sense of relief as I re-checked her and found nothing wrong.

I assured Dr. Tom she was fine, just missing a front tooth. Then he said with such a calming and peace-filled attitude, "Kathy, there's good news and bad news and good news ... but really, it's *all good news.*"

I hesitantly said, "Okay." Good news seemed optimistic.

"Good news is your baby is fine," he shared. "Bad news is, we can't save a tooth in a baby's mouth as there are no roots. Good news is your baby is fine."

He reminded me again how my child had barely missed the huge piece of sheet metal leaning against the door. If that had fallen over and knocked my baby out of her seat she could have had her face or body cut wide open.

Dr. Tom reminded me that Chandra was unharmed except for the loss of one tiny little tooth. And he reminded me of the goodness of God in protecting my child. Everything else seemed inconsequential. But he made me look at the positive. He chose the attitude of gratitude and asked me to don that same attitude as well.

Do you see his attitude? Do you understand his attitude? Would that have been your attitude? A terrible situation, but he saw the good, minimized the bad, and focused on the good. He chose his attitude and it permeated every ounce of my being.

> Will we observe with eyes that see the good in things, trust God in things, and hope for better things?

He finished our conversation and said, "She'll be a cutie, and everyone will think her tooth didn't come in yet. Then they'll think it fell out and she's waiting for her adult tooth. Make the best out of it and remember ... your baby's fine! You're okay. It's going to be all right." He hung up the phone, but his attitude remained with us.

For the next five years, we saw our child in a different light. We saw her face as a blessing. Never missing a tooth, just being missed by tragedy.

God was with us that day, but how do we normally respond when things aren't perfect? When accidents happen, when we don't get our way, when things are changing, shifting and turning, what is our attitude?

Scriptures tell us, *"For I know the plans I have for you ... everything works together for good ... follow Him and He will direct your paths ... and His ways are greater than our ways."*

If Jesus came to offer us an abundant life, then how we respond to our bumps in the road is important for our personal growth.

Will we have glasses half-empty and feed negativity all the time? Or will we look at things through a positive filter? Will we observe with eyes that see the good in things, trust God in things, and hope for better things?

There are times in my life when I have faced the doors of words such as: *That will never happen. I'll never get better. That job is too much for me. She's never going to succeed. We should just give up.*

How do we break down the doors of negative attitudes? Not just those from others, but the doors of negativity that we lock ourselves. Where are we when God begins to say, *"Stretch your faith. Look a little further. Push past your bad attitudes in front of the door and begin to see Me, find Me, follow Me."*

It seems like we are inundated with a world filled with doors that are blocked with a negative stand on almost everything.

If you're anything like me, you have felt surrounded with the overwhelming power of the words *"never"* or *"I can't."* It's time to change the way you think. It's time to take control of your attitudes. It's time to push them aside and bust down the door of attitude that lies behind *"no, don't, never,* and *can't happen."*

A quote about attitude has been repeated in books, letters, speeches, sermons and blogs, Pastor Chuck Swindoll, author and radio host, said this:

> *"The longer I live, the more I realize the impact of attitude on life.*
>
> *"Attitude, to me, is more important than facts. It is more important than success, than what other people think or say or do. It is more important than appearance, giftedness or skill.*
>
> *"It will make or break a company ... a church ... a home.*
>
> *"The remarkable thing is we have a choice every day regarding the attitude we will embrace for that day.*
>
> *"We cannot change our past ... we cannot change the fact that people will act in a certain way. We cannot change the inevitable.*
>
> *"The only thing we can do is play on the one string we have, and that is our attitude ... I am convinced that life is 10% what happens to me and 90% how I react to it.*
>
> *"And so it is with you ... we are in charge of our attitudes."*

Yes, we are in charge of our attitudes. We have control over them. We decide if we will look negatively or positively at a situation. Will we be positive and faith-filled, or will we be negative and doubting?

This past week, I heard the words *"It'll never happen"* so many times it started creeping into my heart and soul and wielding my attitude. I began to feel down and out. I began to tell myself, "I can't succeed, I won't succeed, it will never happen."

Then I went onto God's Word and read what He says to me ... to you ... to all of us who struggle with believing when the word *"never"* takes precedence over everything else.

John 10:10, *"The thief comes only to steal and kill and destroy; I have come that they may have life, and have it to the full."*

The Message Bible states it like this: *"A thief is only there to steal and kill and destroy. I came so they can have real and eternal life, more and better life than they ever dreamed of."*

Philippians 4:13, *"I can do all things through Christ who strengthens me"* (NKJV).

If you trust Jesus as your Savior, you have the power to overcome negativity. You have the power to think differently. You have the power to let the enemy know he doesn't have a right to discourage you or twist your focus to the negative. You can begin to turn over your attitude to the cross.

I believe God can and will help us grasp, attain and maintain a positive attitude, if we ask Him to help us, and then trust Him to do it.

FIRST: God calls to us through *Opportunity.*
When God puts a door of opportunity in front of us, He is providing

something new, something exciting, and purposeful. How will our attitude affect our outcome?

NEXT: God provides for us through *Obstacles.*

With each door that stands in front of us, there will be obstacles that will keep us from busting through the door. Will we walk away or bust through the obstacles to get the door open?

LASTLY: God waits on us for *Obedience.*

Throughout Scripture, God calls us to be faithful. When our attitudes are negative, that shows God we're not believing in His power for a better result.

It's a bad reflection on God and our relationship with Him when we're doubting, when we're worried, and when we're negative about others or our situations.

No one really likes a complainer. Nobody likes people who are negative. No one is drawn to a person who is fussy.

Webster's Dictionary states that *faith* means, *"firm belief in something for which there is no proof, complete trust, without question."*

Faith means you have a GREAT attitude ... a positive attitude.

Scripture tells us in Proverbs 18:21 that *life* and *death* are in the power of the tongue. It's our attitude that has control over our mouth and our actions.

Psychologist Martin Seligman studied a group of several hundred people. He divided them into groups from most to least optimistic and then those who were faith-filled.

He found that 90% of the most optimistic people were still alive at age 85. But only 34% of the most negative, pessimistic people ever made it to age 85.

Life and death are in the power of the tongue. Our attitudes affect our words. Our attitudes determine our actions. Our actions reveal our amount of faith.

Our tongue reports on our level of faith because scripture tells us in Luke 6:45, *"Out of the overflow of a man's mouth his heart speaks."*

In Numbers 1, Moses led the Israelites out of Egypt, crossed the Red Sea, and they resided in the wilderness. God told Moses He would allow one man from each of the twelve tribes of Israel to help him with leadership.

Look Up: Numbers 1:44
"These were the men counted by Moses and Aaron and the twelve leaders of Israel, each one representing his family."

Moses and his brother, Aaron, counted the men who were older than 20 years, and there were 603,550 of them (excluding those from the Tribe of Levi who took care of the Tabernacle). That's a lot of people to care about!

If we were responsible for the happiness of that many people, we might have an attitude of being overwhelmed. Or perhaps our attitude would be negative as we might think we couldn't handle such a big job! Our attitude comes from our heart. Our heart reveals itself through our mouths. And our mouths can speak words of life or death.

If our attitude remains positive, grateful, and happy no matter what, God is pleased because our heart is resonating with the sounds of faith!

When I was a little girl, I always wondered how my Grandma Thelma could be so happy. She had lost her husband when she was a young

48

mother of two, lost her parents and siblings shortly after that, and had lived through a house fire where she lost all their family's possessions. For a while, she and her children stayed in an old rabbit shack behind their destroyed home.

When I asked her how she remained so positive her entire life, she responded quickly by saying, *"How could I be anything else but happy? The Savior died for me, He gave me eternal life. Now that's something to be happy about!"*

The Israelites didn't have a happy attitude. They didn't care that God was providing manna for them. They came up to the door of opportunity. They faced the door of a new land, filled with milk and honey, that was chosen for them. But unfortunately, bad attitudes blocked their entrance.

The vision of a glass half-empty began for the Israelites.

Look Up: Numbers 11:1
"Now the people complained about their hardships in the hearing of the Lord, and when He heard them His anger was aroused. Then fire from the Lord burned among them and consumed some of the outskirts of the camp."

The Israelites can't get over the fact that they didn't have the food they wanted. They might have had the opportunity to get to the Promised Land, but their obstacle was their bad attitude. They were not displaying a positive attitude. Instead, it was an *attitude of discontent.*

You know it. I know it. It's the attitude that complains "How come I never get the raise? How come he always goes on vacation? Why do they get a new car?"

It's the old 'look at someone else and feel dissatisfied' attitude.

Look Up: Philippians 4:11

"I (Paul) *am not saying this because I am in need, for I have learned to be content whatever the circumstances.*"

Look Up: Numbers 11:21-23

"*Moses said, 'Here I am among six hundred thousand men on foot, and you say, "I will give them meat to eat for a whole month!" Would they have enough if flocks and herds were slaughtered for them? Would they have enough if all the fish in the sea were caught for them?'*

"*The Lord answered Moses, 'Is the Lord's arm too short? Now you will see whether or not what I say will come true for you.'*"

God sent manna, now He was sending quail. Lots of them. God was fed up with the lack of faith and the grumbling.

Look Up: Numbers 11:33

"*But while the meat was still between their teeth and before it could be consumed, the anger of the Lord burned against the people, and He struck them with a severe plague.*"

We must obey God and be faith-filled even in times of adversity. The Israelites didn't obey God. They fussed, fretted and doubted God. How would God challenge your attitude today? Would He see you like one of the Israelites grumbling? Or would He see you being faith-filled, encouraged and obedient?

The grumbling is just starting. But there are more complaints to come that would be dispensed through a negative spirit. The glass wasn't just half empty ... there was no glass at all.

Moses was a great spiritual leader to the Israelites, including his siblings and helpers, Miriam and Aaron. He was to lead them to the Promised Land. They had respect because they were being used and blessed by

God because of their help to Moses.

Unfortunately, a spirit of comparison took over with Moses' sister, Miriam, and his brother, Aaron. What's the attitude blocking the door of the Promised Land now? One of *jealousy and comparison.*

Look Up: Numbers 12:1-2

"Miriam and Aaron began to talk against Moses because of his Cushite wife, for he had married a Cushite. 'Has the Lord spoken only through Moses?' they asked. 'Hasn't he also spoken through us?' And the Lord heard this."

Miriam was listed first, so it's more than likely she was the instigator of the negative attitude. When we have a negative attitude and we start sharing it, the attitude spreads. Although no one likes a negative attitude, it's human nature to be attracted to it and to join in and complain.

Miriam's issue about Moses' wife really wasn't the main issue. Her main issue had nothing to do with Moses being married to a Cushite wife. Instead, she was negative because she felt jealous that God was speaking directly to Moses and had put him in charge.

Jealousy is such an ugly attitude. I've been jealous of others and I've had people jealous of me. I've watched how people have tried to talk negatively about others, spread rumors, and try to get people to side against others.

People who are in the right place with the right attitude will reject gossip and negativity against others because that's what Scripture tells us to do.

Obedience would include having a good attitude. God didn't go along with the bad attitude of Moses' siblings. In Numbers 12, God dealt with Miriam and Aaron for their bad attitudes. Miriam suffered leprosy and was sent out of the camp for seven days. Aaron and Moses must delay travel for the camp until the seven days have passed.

God was still giving the Israelites a chance. The opportunity was great! A new land where they could live, thrive and worship God freely. They just needed to bust down the door.

Look Up: Numbers 13:1-16

"The Lord said to Moses, 'Send some men to explore the land of Canaan, which I am giving to the Israelites. From each ancestral tribe send one of its leaders.'

"So at the Lord's command Moses sent them out from the Desert of Paran. All of them were leaders of the Israelites. These are their names:
from the tribe of Reuben, Shammua son of Zakkur;
from the tribe of Simeon, Shaphat son of Hori;
from the tribe of Judah, Caleb son of Jephunneh;
from the tribe of Issachar, Igal son of Joseph;
from the tribe of Ephraim, Hoshea son of Nun;
from the tribe of Benjamin, Palti son of Raphu;
from the tribe of Zebulun, Gaddiel son of Sodi;
from the tribe of Manasseh (a tribe of Joseph), Gaddi son of Susi;
from the tribe of Dan, Ammiel son of Gemalli;
from the tribe of Asher, Sethur son of Michael;
from the tribe of Naphtali, Nahbi son of Vophsi;
from the tribe of Gad, Geuel son of Maki.

"These are the names of the men Moses sent to explore the land. (Moses gave Hoshea son of Nun the name Joshua.)"

Wait! Where's Joseph? He was one of the twelve sons of Jacob. Joseph is missing, and his two sons, Ephraim and Manasseh are listed instead. The reason is that Joseph's father, Jacob, gave the blessing to Joseph's sons.

Joseph isn't listed because his sons are in his place.

In scripture, when we read people's names being changed by God (Abram to Abraham, Sarai to Sara, Jacob to Israel, Simon to Peter and Saul to Paul), we realize that God has a special relationship with that person. Moses changed the name of *Hoshea* to Joshua because he would become a spiritual heir and lead the people out of their days of wandering and into the Promised Land.

These leaders were capable physically and spiritually to seek out the land of Canaan. Unfortunately, their attitudes ended up not being as capable as God would have desired.

What's the attitude blocking the door of the Promised Land now? One of *jealousy and comparison*. Bad attitudes, negative thinking and a desire to spread them wherever they can are what led the Israelites to stop before the door and walk away.

Look Up: Numbers 13:17-20, 25-28
"When Moses sent them to explore Canaan, he said, 'Go up through the Negev and on into the hill country. See what the land is like and whether the people who live there are strong or weak, few or many. What kind of land do they live in? Is it good or bad? What kind of towns do they live in? Are they unwalled or fortified? How is the soil? Is it fertile or poor? Are there trees in it or not? Do your best to bring back some of the fruit of the land.' (It was the season for the first ripe grapes.)

"At the end of forty days they returned from exploring the land.

"They came back to Moses and Aaron and the whole Israelite community at Kadesh in the Desert of Paran. There they reported to them and to the whole assembly and showed them the fruit of the land. They gave Moses this account: 'We went into the land to which you sent us, and it

does flow with milk and honey! Here is its fruit. But the people who live there are powerful, and the cities are fortified and very large. We even saw descendants of Anak there.'"

Anak was an ancestor of the Anakim. The Bible describes them as very tall descendants of the Nephilim. Other sources refer to them as a race of giants.

Forty days the spies were gone. Searching, snooping, scoping things out, and then they returned to Moses and Aaron to make their report.

They show up, but it was not even a half-empty glass attitude. No, instead the glass was completely missing. Smashed by fears, shards of glass left behind, they began to scare anyone who would listen. "Let's spread some fear, some doubt, some dissention," they thought.

Ten of the twelve spies were quickly focused on the negative. They couldn't do it, shouldn't do it, wouldn't do it. Uh-uh. No way. The strength of the people, the protection over the cities, the size of the giants was too big for them to conquer.

Complain and grumble. Bad attitudes. Doubt, fear, dread, defeat.

The obedience for the Israelites came from Jesus' ancestors, Caleb and Joshua. Joshua was the renamed potential leader whom Moses trusted.

Now, Caleb, from the tribe of Judah, jumped into the storyline and told Moses and Aaron ... wait, I've been there, it's not so bad.

Look Up: Numbers 13:30
"Then Caleb silenced the people before Moses and said, 'We should go up and take possession of the land, for we can certainly do it.'"

Look Up: Numbers 14:6-9

"Joshua son of Nun and Caleb son of Jephunneh, who were among those who had explored the land, tore their clothes and said to the entire Israelite assembly, 'The land we passed through and explored is exceedingly good. If the Lord is pleased with us, He will lead us into that land, a land flowing with milk and honey, and will give it to us. Only do not rebel against the Lord. And do not be afraid of the people of the land, because we will devour them. Their protection is gone, but the Lord is with us. Do not be afraid of them.'"

That's a great attitude. That's a positive attitude. Those are words that are stemming from a heart-attitude that says, "Let me by ... I have a door to bust through."

Caleb, you will note, is from the tribe of Judah. The tribe of Judah is the same lineage of Jesus Christ. Jesus is referred to in Revelation as *"The Lion of the tribe of Judah."* This is a family of never-give-up people. This is a lineage that says, "We don't quit, we don't look at the bleak, we love, we live, we try, and we look to God for help." This lineage leads directly to our Savior, Jesus Christ.

Look Up: Revelation 5:5

"Then one of the elders said to me, 'Do not weep! See, the Lion of the tribe of Judah, the Root of David, has triumphed. He is able to open the scroll and its seven seals.'"

REVIEW THREE STEPS ON HAVING A POSITIVE ATTITUDE:

STEP ONE: God calls to us through *Opportunity.*
God provides doors of opportunities in our lives and calls us to something new.

> **John 10:3,** *"The gatekeeper opens the gate for Him, and the sheep listen to His voice. He calls His own sheep by name and leads them out."*

Ephesians 4:1, *"As a prisoner for the Lord, then, I urge you to live a life worthy of the calling you have received."*

II Thessalonians 2:14, *"He called you to this through our gospel, that you might share in the glory of our Lord Jesus Christ."*

STEP TWO: God provides for us through *Obstacles.*

As we are called to doors, obstacles are in our way. God provides help for us to bust through.

Deuteronomy 31:6, *"Be strong and courageous. Do not be afraid or terrified because of them, for the Lord your God goes with you; He will never leave you nor forsake you."*

Isaiah 26:3, *"You will keep in perfect peace those whose minds are steadfast, because they trust in You."*

Isaiah 41:10, *"So do not fear, for I am with you; do not be dismayed, for I am your God. I will strengthen you and help you; I will uphold you with my righteous right hand."*

STEP THREE: God waits on us for *Obedience.*

In order to live an abundant life, we must obey God and be faith-filled even in trials.

Deuteronomy 11:1, *"Love the Lord your God and keep His requirements, His decrees, His laws and His commands always."*

John 14:15, *"If you love Me, keep My commands."*

Romans 1:5, *"Through Him we received grace and apostleship to call all the Gentiles to the obedience that comes from faith for His name's sake."*

Because of the Israelites' unbelief, God judged them, and they had to spend the next forty years wandering through the wilderness. He also said that anyone who was over the age of twenty, *except* for Caleb and Joshua, would die and never see the Promised Land.

By the time the Israelites crossed the Jordan River, Caleb was 80 years old. Another five years passed beyond that before the various tribes of Israel were assigned land to occupy. Caleb described it years later in the book of Joshua.

Look Up: Joshua 14:7-8
(Caleb said to Joshua) *"I was 40 years old when Moses sent me from Kadesh Barnea to explore the land. And I brought him back a report according to my convictions, but the others who went up with me made the hearts of the people melt with fear. I, however, followed the Lord my God wholeheartedly."*

THREE THINGS WE LEARNED:

LESSON ONE: *Follow God* **to the door with a positive faith-filled attitude.**

> **II Chronicles 16:9,** *"For the eyes of the Lord run to and fro throughout the whole earth, to show Himself strong on behalf of those whose heart is loyal to Him."*

LESSON TWO: *Trust God* **to break through obstacles like doubts, fears, or giants that are in our way.**

> **Job 26:12a, 14,** *"By His power He stilled the sea. Behold, these are but the outskirts of His ways, and how small a whisper do we hear of Him! But the thunder of His power who can understand?"*

LESSON THREE: *Obey God* **because we know that God knows what's best for us and He loves us.**

Romans 8:37, *"In all these things we are more than conquerors through Him who loved us."*

How we respond to everyday life can mean a door of opportunity opening for us, or a door that never gets opened because we doubt, complain, grumble and have a bad attitude.

God calls us to opportunities, helps us through obstacles and waits for us to answer through obedience.

Our attitudes affect our words, our words affect our actions and our actions affect our lives.

I heard a story about a man named Ronnie Barnard. When Ronnie was young he felt the call to attend Bible college and prepare for ministry. He felt God's call deep within his soul. But he had one obstacle in front of that opportunity and it was a big one. He stuttered. Ronnie stuttered so badly that he could barely get his own name out when he met people.

But Ronnie continued to believe that God was offering him an opportunity. He knew he saw an obstacle blocking the door, but Ronnie wanted to obey God's call.

When Ronnie finished his college courses, he learned of a church that was searching for a senior pastor. He called the church that needed a pastor and prepared to interview for the position.

But before Ronnie got there, the college's administration office phoned the church and said that the church wouldn't want to employ Ronnie. They told the church that Ronnie had a terrible problem with stuttering and could not speak.

Before Ronnie arrived, the church phoned him and told him not to bother to show up for the interview.

Ronnie felt overwhelmed with disappointment. The door stood in front of him, the obstacle blocked his way. It would have been so very easy for Ronnie to pick up a bad attitude. He could have blamed the school, blamed the church, or blamed God, but Ronnie didn't choose that attitude. Instead, Ronnie told himself he wasn't going to give up. He would obey God. He would believe that with God, he could do anything!

Ronnie had door after door close in his face. He believed that God called him, and God would provide an opportunity. Ronnie would rise above the obstacles and believe.

One day a little church whose congregation was older, dwindling in numbers, and uncertain it could even stay open, called Ronnie and asked him to apply for their pastoral position. They said, "Let's take a chance on him. What can we lose?" They hired Ronnie.

Ronnie could hardly say hello to people without stuttering, but he trusted God, and remained positive. With his faith and positive attitude, God honored that! When Ronnie stood up on the stage to preach, God came through. Ronnie did not stutter at all, but instead, spoke fluently with the anointing power of the Holy Spirit.

Today Ronnie has a mega church of 10,000 people and has planted hundreds of churches throughout Africa.

God asked Ronnie to be faith-filled and obedient. He asked him to remain positive in the faith that says I can't do it ... but God can. Because God helps break through the obstacles, knocks down the doors, and walks you through to your opportunity, you become a door buster, just like Joshua and Caleb. Just like Ronnie Barnard.

Today, you may have walls blocking you, armies against you or giants who are bigger than you. But God is the giver of abundant life and wants to lead you to bust down the doors of a bad attitude. Just believe.

Look around you ... the glass isn't half-empty ... it's overflowing.

Questions:

1. Do you think the Israelites were unreasonable wanting to go back to slavery in Egypt because they missed some of the food they had experienced? Name a time when you wanted to return to a place or relationship that held you back. Did you go back to it? If so, what was it that pulled you back?

2. The ten spies held a negative attitude and completely forgot about God's desire to lead them to the Promised Land. Joshua and Caleb delivered a positive attitude where Caleb described it as one that "followed God wholeheartedly." Name a time when you had a positive attitude about an opportunity. Describe the end results of the situation.

3. Look at your attitude today, how do you typically respond to people and events around you? Would you describe yourself as someone who sees things with a positive half-full attitude, or someone with a negative half-empty attitude?

4. Describe a time when you had a negative attitude towards an opportunity in your life and the bad attitude created trouble for you. What did you learn from that experience?

Look Up: ─

1. **Proverbs 4:23**

2. **Proverbs 17:22**

3. **Matthew 7:11**

4. **Matthew 15:11**

5. **Luke 12:25**

6. **Ephesians 4:31-32**

7. **Philippians 4:8**

Songs:

Hymn ~ *"I Surrender All"* (Words by Judson W. Van DeVenter and Music by Winfield S. Weeden)

Contemporary ~ *"Happy Day"* (Tim Hughes)

Closing Prayer:

Dear Jesus,

Help me to know that You will lead me
through obstacles and call me
to obedience.

I will bring an attitude of praise to You.

I will bring an attitude of obedience
to Your throne.
From everlasting to everlasting,
You are our God.

In Jesus' Name, *Amen.*

Lesson Four

David's Door: Insurmountable Challenges

*"If the Lord be with us, we have no cause of fear.
His eye is upon us, His arm over us,
His ear open to our prayer -
His grace sufficient, His promise unchangeable."*

John Newton

Door Busted: In the last lesson, we learned from Moses that how we respond to everyday life can mean a door of positive attitude opening for us. Or our response can be a door that never gets opened because we doubt, complain, grumble and have a bad attitude. God wants to give us an abundant life and leads us to bust down the doors of bad attitudes that dishonor Him.

Proverbs 3:5-6, *"Trust in the Lord with all your heart and lean not unto your own understanding. In all your ways acknowledge Him and He will direct your paths."*

I remember the day like it was yesterday. I had received the news that my spouse at the time was running a crystal meth lab with his best friend.

The police officer who spoke with me about it told me that the authorities were moving in to make an arrest. He thought I had about two weeks to choose what I would do with my life.

I remember the kind face, the gentle eyes, and the calm voice that spoke directly to me. Detective Jack stated, "I'm not much of a religious man, but I'm telling you this, I'd start praying right now for help from God, and I'd get myself and my children out for safety. If you don't, and they find drugs on your property, your car or your house, your children will be put into foster care and you will be considered an accomplice."

I was stunned. I felt as though my life was crashing in around me. The terror continued.

That night I waited up until 3:00 a.m. for my spouse to return home. His personality was so different, so extreme, that I hardly recognized him. The stronger drugs were keeping him irritable, anxious, paranoid and his eyes looked crazy.

I made myself stay awake. I knew that with his untrustworthy behavior, my children and I were no longer safe. I was paralyzed with fear and didn't know what to do next. I told myself to take one moment at a time.

He pushed through the door loudly. Abrupt sarcasm was tossed my way with every comment. I quietly asked where he'd been. With a strong force that I had not seen, he picked me up and slammed me down against the staircase. I felt my arm hit the wall and my back skid against the side of a stair step.

I looked into his eyes and realized a basic truth that I didn't want to grasp ... he no longer resembled the man I had married twenty years before. He turned me around with my arms held behind my back and whispered vehemently, "I should kill you right now." And that was it for me. Fear crept in like a rapidly-growing vine around my being and reached all the way up to my throat. I could barely swallow.

The only sound I could hear was my shallow breathing. My arms, still pinned behind me, ached, and I wanted to give up. But something happened.

In those moments that seemed like hours, my middle daughter, Chandra, stood at the top of the stairs and said, "Let go of her or I'm calling the police." The crazed trance was broken and he shoved me towards the kitchen door.

Waking up the next morning, I knew that I had to get my children and myself out of this house and quickly. I went to my pastor and elders for help.

The eight men sat around me in a circle. They listened to my story of our abuse and the most recent abuse the night before. I revealed my bruises on my arms and shoulder. They remained firm and emotionless.

I continued to tell them about the upcoming arrest, and the head elder said these words: "If you leave him, you do not have a job. We do not condone divorce under any circumstances. Effective immediately, you are no longer leading worship until you make a decision. Choose wisely."

My legs felt weak with the fear that was now becoming a constant emotion. It had wrapped its choking vine around my soul and was pressing in. I could not eat, I could not sleep, I could not think straight.

Fear had taken over every part of my life. I wanted to lie down and give in. The fear began with threats from my spouse and my boss. The door to freedom from challenges seemed to beckon me. Thoughts of losing the love of my children, job, car, and home, plus the fear of what others would think made a home in my mind.

The challenges seemed insurmountable. In order to break the fear, break the bondage, and be set free, I had to face the giants. The five stones and slingshot David used to slay a giant wouldn't work for me.

I needed a strategic plan. I needed help from God and from humans. I prayed and devised a plan. But it would take much strength and courage to face the challenges that seemed liked giants, and a great deal of help from God and friends.

The challenges that I faced were difficult. They were emotionally, physically, spiritually and mentally draining. Each time I would pick up energy or strength, I would easily become overwhelmed with the next step, the next thing, the next problem.

First, I would need a job. Then, I'd need a place to live. I wondered where I could find a car I could afford and how I would sell the new SUV I owned.

I woke up each day to the mounds of work in decision-making, in peace-making, and in comfort-making. My to-do lists were long and peppered my mind.

My children would need to change schools if I changed jobs and living quarters. Without money, since ours had been squandered on drugs, I wondered how I could afford any place to live.

One cold winter morning I felt so alone that I laid on the kitchen floor next to a mountain of laundry. Dirt, stains, smells, and an overwhelming amount of mess stretched out next to me. I remember thinking that this pile represented my life. Insurmountable mountains, giants of fear. I didn't know how to face them, couldn't begin to believe they would all work out, and an overwhelming urge to cry all the time enveloped me.

The last thing I ever imagined was being divorced. After twenty years of putting up with abuse in every manner of the word, the pain that went along with that abuse seemed nothing in comparison to the challenges that were mounting up in front of me.

Life is constantly made up of things that create comfort and peace, encouragement and pleasure, contentment and happiness. But it is also consistently made up of things that create trouble and hardship, along with pain and hurt. Anxiety and fear will creep in over and over. Your pain can grow and start to become mountains that you cannot cross, valleys that seem too deep, and giants that cannot be conquered.

How we handle our challenges is where we meet God. I believe it's one of the most crucial lessons to learn in life. I believe we must re-learn it frequently, as we tend to forget.

Do we remain shocked and frozen as I frequently did in the memories I just relayed? Do we recoil from whatever is scaring us? Do we create an attitude of denial or avoidance? How do we handle things that make us fearful and afraid?

> How we handle our challenges is where we meet God.

As I learned about what I thought were my insurmountable challenges, I learned about fear.

FIVE THINGS WE FEAR THE MOST:
As the years go by the things you fear may change, but the top five remain constant.

1. **Fear of dying**

2. **Fear of being alone**

3. **Fear of public speaking**

4. **Fear of failure**

5. **Fear of rejection**

Apparently, *fear of divorce* and what comes after that didn't rate the top five list. *But it was my entire list!*

Webster's Dictionary states that *fear* means, *"An unpleasant feeling of anxiety or apprehension caused by the presence or anticipation of danger."* When we think we're in trouble, we become afraid. It's a normal human behavioral pattern. But at times, we can become afraid and the fear may last more than a few moments or days. Instead, it moves in front of any opportunity to freedom and takes residence in front of our doors where we are changing our lives forever.

In the story of David and Goliath, from I Samuel 17, we read about how David, who was estimated to be fifteen years old, made his way to take food to his brothers.

But soon afterwards, David discovered trouble in the land. Even the strongest Israelite soldiers were afraid of a Philistine giant named Goliath of Gath *(Gath was one of five city states of the Philistines)*.

The story begins with David, born in Bethlehem in the land of Judah. David was only ten generations removed from Judah, one of Jacob's twelve sons and the lineage of Jesus Christ.

In this Bible passage, King Saul and the Israelites were facing the Philistines, the main enemies of Israel. Twice a day for forty days, Goliath, the champion of the Philistines, came out and challenged the Israelites to send out a champion of their own to fight him. King Saul and his army were terrified.

Goliath is reported in the Bible to be "six cubits and a span." This indicates a very big man approximately nine feet nine inches tall. The average size man in those days was about five foot five inches, according to skeletons found in the area during archaeology digs.

David's Door: Insurmountable Challenges

In the Valley of Elah, the Israelites dug in along the northern ridge, and the Philistines dug in along the southern ridge. The two armies camped out for weeks because they were deadlocked. Neither could attack the other, because to attack the other side meant they would have to travel into the valley and then up the other side. Thus, being completely exposed to the enemy.

Look Up: I Samuel 17: 1-7

"Now the Philistines gathered their forces for war and assembled at Sokoh (Sokoh is located 15 miles west of Bethlehem near the Philistine border) *in Judah. They pitched camp at Ephes Dammim, between Sokoh and Azekah. Saul and the Israelites assembled and camped in the Valley of Elah and drew up their battle line to meet the Philistines. The Philistines occupied one hill and the Israelites another, with the valley between them.*

"A champion named Goliath, who was from Gath, came out of the Philistine camp. His height was six cubits and a span. He had a bronze helmet on his head and wore a coat of scale armor of bronze weighing five thousand shekels, on his legs he wore bronze greaves, and a bronze javelin was slung on his back. His spear shaft was like a weaver's rod, and its iron point weighed six hundred shekels. His shield bearer went ahead of him."

The description of Goliath's spear emphasizes that he was a trained and successful warrior. His spear shaft was two inches thick or more, and his spearhead alone weighed 15 pounds. An assistant walked ahead of Goliath carrying a shield. Goliath's bronze helmet, leg armor and a coat of mail weighed about 125 pounds.

There was no doubt in the eyes of the Israelites that this giant was a fierce competitor. It would be highly unlikely that anyone would have strength or power to overcome him, let alone enough courage.

Look Up: I Samuel 17:8-24

"Goliath stood and shouted to the ranks of Israel, 'Why do you come out and line up for battle? Am I not a Philistine, and are you not the servants of Saul? Choose a man and have him come down to me. If he is able to fight and kill me, we will become your subjects; but if I overcome him and kill him, you will become our subjects and serve us.' Then the Philistine said, 'This day I defy the armies of Israel! Give me a man and let us fight each other.' On hearing the Philistine's words, Saul and all the Israelites were dismayed and terrified.

"Now David was the son of an Ephrathite named Jesse, who was from Bethlehem in Judah. Jesse had eight sons, and in Saul's time he was very old. Jesse's three oldest sons had followed Saul to the war: The firstborn was Eliab; the second, Abinadab; and the third, Shammah. David was the youngest. The three oldest followed Saul, but David went back and forth from Saul to tend his father's sheep at Bethlehem.

"For forty days the Philistine came forward every morning and evening and took his stand. Now Jesse said to his son David, 'Take this ephah of roasted grain (about 36 pounds) *and these ten loaves of bread for your brothers and hurry to their camp. Take along these ten cheeses to the commander of their unit. See how your brothers are and bring back some assurance from them. They are with Saul and all the men of Israel in the Valley of Elah, fighting against the Philistines.'*

"Early in the morning David left the flock in the care of a shepherd, loaded up and set out, as Jesse had directed. He reached the camp as the army was going out to its battle positions, shouting the war cry. Israel and the Philistines were drawing up their lines facing each other. David left his things with the keeper of supplies, ran to the battle lines and asked his brothers how they were. As he was talking with them, Goliath, the Philistine champion from Gath, stepped out from his lines and shouted

his usual defiance, and David heard it. Whenever the Israelites saw the man, they all fled from him in great fear."

The Enemy's tactic will always remain the same ... use fear to separate us from our faith in God and His power. He uses our minds to tell us that the challenge is so great, so big, so giant, that we don't want to even attempt to break the door down and walk through it. After all, we are powerless against the giants.

Pastor and bestselling author, Rick Warren wrote, *"Fear is a self-imposed prison that will keep you from becoming what God intends for you to be. You must move against it with the weapons of faith and love."*

We can be lured, taunted and tempted so that we become afraid and believe that our giants are so great they can't be taken down. We become stationary and cannot move forward or accomplish what we need to do for God. We can't bust down any door in front of us.

So often when my team goes out to deliver a conference, we meet with people who are overwhelmed with their challenges. It's too much, it's too great, the problems are gigantic. They're afraid to walk out of an abusive relationship in case they never meet someone else and they're left alone. Or they're afraid to take a new job because they might not be as successful as they are at their current position. Or maybe they're afraid to get married because it will change their independence. It's too much work; they remain on the sidelines and wonder what's behind door number one.

Whatever it is that's making people afraid always ends up holding them back from moving ahead, and many times they are exactly like King Saul and the Israelites. They are on one side of the mountain afraid to move for fear of what may or may not happen. The giants in the land are a fierce foe.

When David learned more about the giant, he was challenged to look into the face of everyone's fear and determine if the obstacle was really insurmountable. David must decide if he can stand up, step up and bust down the door of fear.

Look Up: I Samuel 17:25-28

"Now the Israelites had been saying, 'Do you see how this man keeps coming out? He comes out to defy Israel. The king will give great wealth to the man who kills him. He will also give him his daughter in marriage and will exempt his family from taxes in Israel.'"

Wealth, marriage, and financial freedom are the wonderful blessings behind the door of opportunity. However, the insurmountable challenges in front of the door must be busted through.

"David asked the men standing near him, 'What will be done for the man who kills this Philistine and removes this disgrace from Israel? Who is this uncircumcised Philistine that he should defy the armies of the living God?'

"They repeated to him what they had been saying and told him, 'This is what will be done for the man who kills him.'

"When Eliab, David's oldest brother, heard him speaking with the men, he burned with anger at him and asked, 'Why have you come down here? And with whom did you leave those few sheep in the wilderness? I know how conceited you are and how wicked your heart is; you came down only to watch the battle.'"

The oldest brother, Eliab, accused his little brother, David, of being conceited and wicked. God's opinion of David was far different. God has been, is, and always will be looking for those who are ready to step up and have courage. Later on, God makes David a king.

Look Up: Acts 13:22

"After removing Saul, he made David their king. God testified concerning him: 'I have found David son of Jesse, a man after my own heart; he will do everything I want him to do.'"

But David did not waver with his brother's criticism. Instead, the fear of this giant, the taunting against the Lord irritated David and began to give him strength.

Look Up: I Samuel 17:29-37

"'Now what have I done?' said David. 'Can't I even speak?' He then turned away to someone else and brought up the same matter, and the men answered him as before. What David said was overheard and reported to Saul, and Saul sent for him.

"David said to Saul, 'Let no one lose heart on account of this Philistine; your servant will go and fight him.'"

David stood in front of the door with his insurmountable object ... a giant. He was ready to move forward in obedience and bust down the door.

"Saul replied, 'You are not able to go out against this Philistine and fight him; you are only a young man, and he has been a warrior from his youth.'

"But David said to Saul, 'Your servant has been keeping his father's sheep. When a lion or a bear came and carried off a sheep from the flock, I went after it, struck it and rescued the sheep from its mouth. When it turned on me, I seized it by its hair, struck it and killed it. Your servant has killed both the lion and the bear; this uncircumcised Philistine will be like one of them, because he has defied the armies of the living God. The

Lord who rescued me from the paw of the lion and the paw of the bear will rescue me from the hand of this Philistine.'

"Saul said to David, 'Go, and the Lord be with you.'"

David had no confidence in himself, only a strong, bold confidence in the One who created the door, allowed the giant to stand in front of it, and now waited for David's response.

David felt the need to prove himself with a short history lesson of his life for the King.

However, there was more to King Saul's offer in these scriptures than just a gesture of kindness for protection for the young David. During this era, positions of authority were marked by formal insignia or by special clothing. The ruler's weapon, typically a sword, was seen as a gift of the deities and a mark of favor.

Israelite culture considered the transfer of clothing as the transfer of status. When the King offered David his armor, Saul offered David his position as king of Israel. David was ready to bust down the door, however he was not going to commit to the clothing swap.

Although the sword was a mark of his position as defender of Israel, David couldn't wear the armor or the sword. He was not ready to rule the land even though he had the favor of God and the courage to defend Israel against a giant.

Later on, David would become king when Saul's son, Jonathan, covenanted with David and the gesture of transferring the king's clothing and armor was completed.

Look Up: I Samuel 17:38-49
"Then Saul dressed David in his own tunic. He put a coat of armor on

him and a bronze helmet on his head. David fastened on his sword over the tunic and tried walking around, because he was not used to them. 'I cannot go in these,' he said to Saul, 'because I am not used to them.' So he took them off. Then he took his staff in his hand, chose five smooth stones from the stream, put them in the pouch of his shepherd's bag and, with his sling in his hand, approached the Philistine."

It was a normal piece of equipment for shepherds to carry a sling to ward off wild animals that threatened their flock. The sling was a hollow pocket of leather attached to two cords. A stone would be placed in the pocket, the shepherd would swing it around to gain momentum, would release one cord and hurl it at the predator. Theologians believe the stones were the size of a baseball.

Theologians have tried to determine why five stones were taken to the battlefield. After all, if he had faith in God, wouldn't he just need one? But it doesn't really matter that he took five. Perhaps they were to be prepared for the brothers and another giant mentioned in scripture, or maybe it was to battle anyone else who would step out into battle against him. Nevertheless, David took out only one stone and prepared for battle.

"Meanwhile, the Philistine, with his shield bearer in front of him, kept coming closer to David. He looked David over and saw that he was little more than a boy, glowing with health and handsome, and he despised him. He said to David, 'Am I a dog, that you come at me with sticks?' And the Philistine cursed David by his gods. 'Come here,' he said, 'and I'll give your flesh to the birds and the wild animals!'

"David said to the Philistine, 'You come against me with sword and spear and javelin, but I come against you in the name of the Lord Almighty, the God of the armies of Israel, whom you have defied. This day the Lord will

deliver you into my hands, and I'll strike you down and cut off your head. This very day I will give the carcasses of the Philistine army to the birds and the wild animals, and the whole world will know that there is a God in Israel. All those gathered here will know that it is not by sword or spear that the Lord saves; for the battle is the Lord's, and He will give all of you into our hands.'

"As the Philistine moved closer to attack him, David ran quickly toward the battle line to meet him. Reaching into his bag and taking out a stone, he slung it and struck the Philistine on the forehead. The stone sank into his forehead, and he fell face down on the ground."

Five smooth stones from the stream were all that David armed himself with physically. Spiritually, he had the power of the Almighty God of Abraham, Isaac and Jacob accompanying him that day. David was not worried; his strength overpowered the giant.

Holocaust survivor, Corrie Ten Boom encourages us as we saw David overcoming his fear, *"Worry does not empty tomorrow of its sorrow, it empties today of its strength."*

At times we might feel like our fears are completely founded. Maybe cancer is taking over your body or someone is threatening you physically. Perhaps you are afraid of the debt that has taken over, you're losing your job and you won't be able to afford your lifestyle.

Whatever our trials are, they always are very real to us. They become insurmountable challenges that seem to be giant. We may feel hopeless to defeat them or change our future.

David embraced the emotion of anger and irritation he felt against Goliath and used it as a powerful tool to help take down the giant. He also used his strong faith in our Heavenly Father and was propelled forward. He put his faith in God's power, not his own, as he faced the door.

Theologians might have their ideas about the stones, but I believe that David's five smooth stones represent the tools that God wants us to use when battling the enemy and our fears. When facing the obstacles that keep us from busting our way through, we can use these stones.

FIVE STONES OF FAITH:

1. **Faith in God**

2. **Insight from the prayers and help of others**

3. **Perseverance to formulate and carry out a plan**

4. **Strength created from emotions**

5. **Wisdom found in God's Word**

Look Up: I Samuel 17:50
"So David triumphed over the Philistine with a sling and a stone; without a sword in his hand he struck down the Philistine and killed him."

Scripture says that David was a man after God's own heart. God knew he would do what was necessary to obey Him. He knew David would not give in to fear, he would not be bullied, and he would not be manipulated by others who tried to make him feel afraid.

One morning I stood in front of my children's father and let him know that I was taking our three daughters and moving out. Glaring at me, taunting me, he mocked me. He told me that I would never have another job working for a church, I would never be loved, and I would never be free of him. He hoped to create fear around me and make the giants look bigger.

In those moments of facing my giants, I began to feel dizzy. I began to think, "He's right ... I can't do it." And all of a sudden, I felt the heaviness of the armor that was too big for me. I began to recite in my mind that it was easier to just give up, to give in and quit.

The giants were being rattled off one by one. No job, no home, no car, no one to love, no one who'd love me—all became bigger and bigger.

But deep inside as the challenges tossed and turned about, I remembered the *stone of strength* that God had promised me if I only trusted in Him. I remembered the promise of my mother and father, who were on their way from southwest Iowa to help me. I remembered the *stone of prayers* from my friends.

I looked him straight in the eyes and took out my *stone of faith*. I hurled it as hard as I could when I said these words, "Perhaps it will be bigger than I can handle. Perhaps I will not find love and not be free. But I will never know unless I trust God and take that first step. Goodbye." I walked out the front door and never returned.

Before that last conversation, I made a phone call to a church thirty minutes away that was looking for a worship director. The pastor listened intently as I explained I had served as a worship director for many years and would love to apply for the job. I revealed a few obstacles in the way—I was divorcing, and my family was needing help. He paused for one second and asked me, "How soon can you get here?"

I knew that this was the *perseverance stone of planning* to bust down the door. I drove into the city and looked up at the water tower. It proudly displayed the name of the small city. Amidst the dark, bleak day that had produced thunder, lightning and huge cold raindrops, I saw the sky clearing. It was a strange sight. The sun shone down on the water tower and I heard God clearly speak to my soul, "This will be a place of help, hope and healing."

After the job interview that lasted for exactly one hour, the kind pastor offered me the position as worship director. I told no one.

I returned to my church to announce my resignation. The elders and pastor informed me I'd never get another job and I had to stay married or I would be under punishment from God for the rest of my life. They taunted and harassed.

As I packed my boxes, I focused on the *stone of wisdom* from God's word found in Proverbs 19:8, *"The one who gets wisdom loves life; the one who cherishes understanding will soon prosper."* Focused on God, I turned off the lights, walked out of that church and never looked back. The next step to bust down the door would be to face the giants of my daughters' safety, where to live, find a car, and enroll my kids in a new school.

When I started my new position ten days later, I was met with love, protection, and provision. My children and I were safe. The giants were defeated. *The five smooth stones of faith had been used against the Enemy.*

What the Enemy intended for evil, God meant for good.

The first thing that happens when we're overwhelmed with troubles that seem to look like giants, is that we become blurry-brained. We don't know what to say, where to go, what to do. We're overcome with confusion.

The second thing that happens is that we want to give up and quit. We believe we can't make our way out of the mess, so we just sit in it. Accept it. Keep living outside the door of freedom from insurmountable challenges.

The next thing that happens is that we continue on the merry-go-round of the prison of our complacency and life stays the same or gets worse.

In order to break the bonds of sin, whether it is self-induced or is someone else's sin imposed on you, you need to go directly to the cross. Jesus is the only one who can help you. The great part about getting help from Jesus is that He paid for the sins of the world when He died on the cross.

The Enemy wants us to believe that we are defeated, stuck, and unable to break through the bondage. Getting us to believe his lies is his greatest ploy.

FOUR STEPS TO BUST THROUGH DOORS:
How can you get up and move towards that door, brush past obstacles and bust down doors?

STEP ONE: *Admit* **your need for help.**
Be humble and honest and go before God confessing any sin and admitting your need.

> **Proverbs 28:13,** *"Whoever conceals their sins does not prosper, but the one who confesses and renounces them finds mercy."*

> **James 4:10,** *"Humble yourselves before the Lord, and He will lift you up."*

> **I John 1:9,** *"If we confess our sins, He is faithful and just and will forgive us our sins and purify us from all unrighteousness."*

STEP TWO: *Address* **your needs specifically.**
Once you go before God, let Him know each and every need you have and ask for help.

> **Romans 8:32,** *"He who did not spare His own Son but gave Him up for us all, how will He not also with Him graciously give us all*

things?"

Philippians 4:6, *"Do not be anxious about anything, but in every situation, by prayer and petition, with thanksgiving, present your requests to God."*

Philippians 4:19, *"And my God will supply every need of yours according to His riches in glory in Christ Jesus."*

STEP THREE: *Accept* the help God sends.

God will send help through neighbors, friends, family, the church, and even strangers.

James 1:17, *"Every good and perfect gift is from above, coming down from the Father of the heavenly lights, who does not change like shifting shadows."*

Jeremiah 29:11, *"For I know the plans I have for you, declares the Lord, plans for welfare and not for evil, to give you a future and a hope."*

Matthew 21:22, *"And whatever you ask in prayer, you will receive, if you have faith."*

STEP FOUR: *Arm* yourself with protection.

The Enemy wants you to be unable to get to freedom. Once free, prepare yourself to stay that way!

Psalm 5:11, *"But let all who take refuge in You be glad; let them ever sing for joy. Spread Your protection over them, that those who love Your name may rejoice in You."*

Isaiah 41:10, *"So do not fear, for I am with you; do not be dismayed, for I am your God. I will strengthen you and help you; I will uphold you with my righteous right hand."*

II Thessalonians 3:3, *"But the Lord is faithful, and He will strengthen you and protect you from the evil one."*

The giants of challenges will seem as big as you let them. Take one thing at a time, one day at a time, one step at a time.

Through the power of Jesus, you will be able to bust the door of each giant challenge. Trust in His power, in His strength, in His care.

Remind yourself that giving in isn't an option. David did not give up or give in. Instead, as a young man, he believed he could take down the giant, even though others around him who were more skilled could not.

Equip yourself with the five stones of faith and follow the steps. Know that it will never be about you and your strength. It's only about God and His strength. He gives you the strength, the answers, and the help when you are humble enough to seek Him and ask for help.

Look Up: I Samuel 17:45
"David said to the Philistine, 'You come against me with sword and spear and javelin, but I come against you in the name of the Lord Almighty, the God of the armies of Israel, whom you have defied.'"

It will never be easy to face what we think are the insurmountable challenges, but God is with us, just as He was with David. You might feel overcome, but you are an overcomer!

I love this quote from Pastor Chuck Swindoll.

> *"We must cease striving and trust God to provide what He thinks is best and in whatever time He chooses to make it available. But this kind of trusting doesn't come naturally. It's a spiritual crisis of the will in which we must choose to*

exercise faith."

When you feel that fear is creeping into the nooks and crannies of your soul, it's time to get out the five stones of faith and put them into place.

God doesn't ever leave us. We do not walk through things alone.

Look Up: Deuteronomy 31:6
"Be strong and courageous. Do not be afraid or terrified because of them, for the Lord your God goes with you; He will never leave you nor forsake you."

Meet with God, create your plan, grab your slingshot and your five smooth stones and head out into life. It's calling you. Don't be afraid. The giants aren't really all they seem to be. With God's help, like Goliath, they fall.

Questions:

1. Thinking about this past week, name one challenge that you had to face. How did you stop the fear and what happened?

2. Do you have a fear that has established residency within your heart and mind? Name that fear and one small step you could take to overcome it.

3. Have you ever used any of the five faith stones when dealing with an insurmountable challenge? If so, which ones have you used? Do you have any others that were not mentioned?

4. Have you ever had anyone taunt, tease and try to surround you with fear? How have you responded?

Look Up:

1. Joshua 1:9

2. Psalm 23.4

3. Psalm 94:19

4. Isaiah 35:4

5. Matthew 6:24

6. John 14:27

7. II Timothy 1:7

Songs:

Hymn ~ *"How Great Thou Art"* (Carl Boberg)

Contemporary ~ *"One Thing Remains"* (Brian Johnson, Jeremy Riddle and Christa Black Gifford)

Closing Prayer:

Dear Jesus,
When I am afraid, I pray
that I will release my fears to You.

I pray that You will give me
divine wisdom
to handle the situation.

Help me remember that You
are constantly with me,
and that no giant is too big for You.

Strengthen me and give me Your peace.

In Jesus' Name, *Amen.*

Lesson Five

Elijah's Door: Fear of Social Pressures

"Courage is contagious.
When a brave man takes the stand,
the spines of others are often stiffened."

Billy Graham

Door Busted: In our last lesson, we learned that David faced insurmountable challenges. When we face challenges, God wants us to remember and rely on His strength and not our own. He gives us the strength, the answers, the help when we are humble enough to seek Him and ask Him for help.

Proverbs 13:20, *"Walk with the wise and become wise, for a companion of fools suffers harm."*

When I was a teenager, I had a friend named Sherrie *(name changed to protect her identity)*. Sherrie was always a little different, a little louder than others, a little bit more awkward. But Sherrie had a huge heart, a kind soul, and an incredible musical gift.

I think the bullying Sherrie experienced started in junior high. The sweet controlled days of one-room classes in elementary school ended and the tormenting began.

It was fall and school had just started when I began to watch it happen. Big ninth grade boys were pushing her, and her books would fly all over the hallway. Girls would pass by and whisper about her handmade clothing, her kinky hair, or her little round black glasses. Teachers would become exasperated with her loud answers and her bossy mannerisms. However, there was just something about Sherrie that made me drawn to her.

One day, she took the stage at the end of our music class. The auditorium felt immense as our music teacher auditioned kids for the talent show. The rows of chairs were filled with students who giggled, whispered, and acted unruly.

Sherrie grabbed the microphone while the teacher played the introduction to the "Sound of Music." I'd never heard the song, but I loved Sherrie's voice, her inflections, and her dramatic delivery. When she finished the audition, I was so enraptured in the moment, I stood up and clapped. Within seconds I realized I was the only one. Others glared, looked at me with shock and several called out, "Sit down!"

I couldn't understand why so many people didn't like her. She was smart, funny, loud—yes, but everything else that was good and endearing overpowered her quirks. That day, I determined that I wanted her for a friend.

A few days later I caught up with Sherrie while she was going to her next class. I congratulated her on getting included in the talent show. She smiled, giggled, and asked, "Will you try out as well?" I was elated that she even knew I loved music and singing.

For the next few weeks, I walked with Sherrie to classes and the lunch room, while people whispered and glared. I sat with her while people gossiped and giggled. Finally, it was the last day for try-outs for the show. Sherrie asked me if I would sing a duet with her. She asked if she could sing harmony while I sang the lead to "The Sound of Silence," by Simon and Garfunkel. I knew the song well and happily accepted the invite.

Being skilled musicians, without practice, we stood up and sang the song. Much to my surprise, *the sound of silence* covered the auditorium like a big, dark blanket. No one giggled, no one whispered. To Sherrie and me it seemed as though *no one dared disturb the sound of silence.*

Slowly one lone friend began to clap and then another and another. The teacher smiled approvingly and marked us on the list as a part of the show.

I ran home to tell my mother that I was singing a duet with Sherrie. Mom knew Sherrie's family and she was pleased. I told my mother about my fear of peer pressure. "No one likes her, Mom," I confided. "I think that if I am her friend, they will not like me."

Mom poured a big, cold glass of milk, handed me a sunflower seed cookie and answered in her smart-mom fashion, "It doesn't matter what they think. You're living your life. If you want her for a friend, she's a nice girl, I'd be her friend. She needs you more than you need her, Kathy."

Sherrie called me that night and told me her mother was sewing us matching jumpsuits in a robin's egg blue color. Her mother was so thankful that she had a friend, she was going to do everything she could to appreciate me. I felt humbled and a little nervous for the backlash I knew would be coming.

Another night went by when I started getting phone calls. A couple of crank calls making fun of me. And a few calls where "friends" ridiculed, "Don't do it. You have a great voice, a great reputation. She's weird. No one likes her. You absolutely can't sing with her or become her friend. It will be the end of you."

I prayed and weighed it before God and my parents. I made the decision that I would be her friend. I would sing the duet.

Something strange started happening after that event. Instead of people being mean to me, they were starting to be kind to Sherrie. Instead of pushing and threatening, others began to see her like I saw her.

Sherrie grew up and continued to remain a little bit unusual. Now, years later, those same people who bullied, pushed, and harassed Sherrie are her friends on social media. They probably don't even remember how they treated her. She took a job in ministry and diligently serves—loving God and loving people. Somehow the peer pressure made things better and didn't make Sherrie bitter.

But do things always turn out that way? How do we respond in our everyday lives when we're faced with pressure from others? What happens when we face pressure to do things we wouldn't normally do, act a way we shouldn't, or say things that God wouldn't want us to say?

Scripture tells us in Romans 12:2, *"Do not conform to the pattern of this world, but be transformed by the renewing of your mind. Then you will be able to test and approve what God's will is—His good, pleasing and perfect will."*

There will be times in our lives when we see a door of opportunity and it's blocked by the obstacles of social pressure and what others might think. I have known people throughout my life who didn't take jobs, didn't marry someone, didn't move away, and didn't become who they should have become, all because they were afraid of what people might think.

My father used to tell me, "Kathleen, think about where you're at right now in life. Now, fast track to five years from now. Will it matter to others what you did? How does that really concern or affect them? Why is that so important?"

What I learned from those engaging questions was simply that we are living our own life. We get to choose. Don't stop in front of the door because you're afraid of bullying and peer pressure. Sometimes the greatest pressures in life hold us back from the greatest outcomes.

Everywhere we look, today's society is becoming increasingly pushy when it comes to peer pressure. We can turn on the news at any given moment and see major news stations presenting sour attitudes.

Throughout history people have displayed great respect for our country, our flag, our armed forces and our president. Now, when people are supportive of these honorable things, they are bullied and pressured to believe that there is something wrong with them. They're ridiculed for their patriotism!

> Sometimes the greatest pressures in life hold us back from the greatest outcomes.

Football players who make millions of dollars to run back and forth and throw a ball are refusing to respect our country. We have lost our sense of entertainment, as it's become a political hot seat.

Children attending public schools today are forced to listen to and agree that the norm of life we once knew, between a mother and father, is no longer the only ideal that is acceptable. The moral compass that directs us to right and wrong has been smashed and is now different from what the Bible states in clear terms.

Colleges are experiencing knock-down, drag-out fights between teachers and students who don't agree with the majorities' opinions. Many conservative speakers trying to share their viewpoints at liberal schools are beaten, threatened and blocked from sharing their thoughts and concerns at those college campuses.

Angry mobs are violently and brutally injuring innocent lives, demolishing property, and screaming profanities. What starts out as quiet protests, turns to rage.

All of this points to one thing: *peer pressure*. If you don't agree with others who have the louder voice, you are susceptible to violence. Maybe you're not pushed or have your books knocked out of your hand, but instead, in today's society, there are much more serious ramifications. At times, and in certain places, you can be in danger of being harmed or even killed if you don't agree with the majority and their mobs of protestors.

Former President Ronald Reagan once stated, *"Above all, we must realize that no arsenal, or no weapon in the arsenals of the world, is so formidable as the will and moral courage of free men and women. It is a weapon our adversaries in today's world do not have."*

Yet, are we really free to express our thoughts, opinions and choices when we don't agree with others? We might think that this is a problem for the 21st century only. But as we study scripture, we see that history repeats itself. In the instance of the prophet Elijah, King Ahab and Queen Jezebel, there was a lot of peer pressure, bullying, and even killing going on in the northern Jewish nation of Israel.

The story begins with an evil King Ahab, and his very evil wife Queen Jezebel.

Look Up: I Kings 16:30

"Ahab son of Omri did more evil in the eyes of the Lord than any of those before him."

If that leader was already known for his evil, whatever he was pressuring others to do, wouldn't be upright and Godly.

Look Up: I Kings 16:31

"He not only considered it trivial to commit the sins of Jeroboam son of Nebat, but he also married Jezebel daughter of Ethbaal king of the Sidonians, and began to serve Baal and worship him."

The Phoenicians, another name for Sidonians, lived on the Mediterranean coast in the cities of Tyre and Sidon. King Ahab determined he needed to create an alliance with the nations that neighbored northern Israel. Ahab made a treaty with the king of Phoenicia and married his daughter, Jezebel. Jezebel moved to Samaria, the capital of Israel.

Because Jezebel wasn't Jewish and didn't follow God and His commandments, she brought her Canaanite gods with her to Samaria. She had grown up worshiping Baal and Asherah and was determined to remove the worship of God throughout northern Israel.

By means of force and peer pressure, Queen Jezebel replaced all of the worship of the true God in Israel with her gods Baal and Asherah. Anyone who worshiped God, including the prophets of God, were threatened, bullied, beaten, and killed.

Before the reign of Ahab and Jezebel, the prophets of God were always untouched and protected. Their rule and threats, along with peer pressure, was so powerful that no one was beyond their horrific control.

During this time, the God-seeking prophet Elijah, whose name means *my God is the Lord*, began his ministry. Theologians believe that Elijah served in his role as a prophet about 865-850 BC.

Look Up: I Kings 17:1
"Now Elijah the Tishbite, from Tishbe (a village on what is now Jordan's side of the Jordan River) *in Gilead, said to Ahab, 'As the Lord the God of Israel, lives, whom I serve, there will be neither dew, nor rain in the next few years except at my word.'"*

At that time, living water was strongly associated with the presence of God. Elijah would show everyone that God was not blessing this horrific peer pressure, bullying and slaughter of God's prophets. This created a problem for Ahab and Jezebel.

From Genesis to Revelation, Scripture speaks of living water. In the Middle East, where the story took place, water was *(and still is)* scarce, precious, and needed for survival. Rain only fell a few months of the year in Israel, and the rest of the time the ancient peoples survived on stagnant water that was stored in cisterns in the ground. Without rainfall, the royals knew they would have trouble.

The difference with or without rain in Israel was astonishing. The hills could be barren and brown for much of the year, but after some rain, they were covered in green meadows and flowers. Where there were rivers, lush vegetation surrounded them, while only yards away, barren land was prevalent. Water was essential for life and growth and they believed their god would provide it! But with Elijah's decree, there was a drought in the land for nearly three years.

Another problem for the King and Queen? Their god, Baal, was supposed to be the *god of nature—the rain god*. He was in charge of the fertility of flock, field, and family. Elijah's statement, recorded in I Kings 17:1, stated that he alone had control over the weather. Ahab and Jezebel were uncertain about how to deal with him. Their god's lack of power over the drought caused them to become angry.

Look Up: I Kings 18:17-21

"When he saw Elijah, he (King Ahab) *said to him, 'Is that you, you trouble maker of Israel?'*

'I have not made trouble for Israel,' Elijah replied. 'But you and your father's family have. You have abandoned the Lord's commands and have followed the Baals. Now summon the people from all over Israel to meet me on Mount Carmel. And bring the four hundred and fifty prophets of Baal and the four hundred prophets of Asherah, who eat at Jezebel's table.'

"So Ahab sent word throughout all Israel and assembled the prophets on Mount Carmel. Elijah went before the people and said, 'How long will you waver between two opinions? If the Lord is God, follow Him; but if Baal is God, follow him.'

"But the people said nothing."

There was a doorway for the people. It was a doorway of hope and life. It was a doorway that said worship God and be fulfilled. But peer pressure was in the way. Threatening, violent pressure that said, "Don't do it!"

It's a challenging role we experience when we're pressured to do something. If you have become used to being bullied, sometimes you just back down and remain quiet. Retreating can be your habit, your go-to form of action. Sometimes you just give up, give in, and go along with the bullies.

At this point in the story, the people were terrified that they would be included in the mass murders of the prophets whom Jezebel killed. If people didn't choose to follow her gods, her peer pressure served as the ultimate pressure—*death*.

Look Up: I Kings 18:22-24

"Then Elijah said to them, 'I am the only one of the Lord's prophets left, but Baal has four hundred and fifty prophets. Get two bulls for us. Let Baal's prophets choose one for themselves, and let them cut it into pieces and put it on the wood but not set fire to it. I will prepare the other bull and put it on the wood but not set fire to it. Then you call on the name of your god, and I will call on the name of the Lord. The god who answers by fire—he is God.'

"Then all the people said, 'What you say is good.'"

It was time to face the door. It was time to push aside the peer pressures of the powerful political leaders and bust down that door. Fear is conquered when we put our trust in God. Will people despise us, reject us, make fun of us? Will they bully and make threats? What's that to you and me when God has set the door in front of us?

Elijah was going to push up his sleeves and get ready for God's power. How can we tap into the power of the Almighty? Through the power of prayer, through faith, and through the Holy Spirit. Elijah knew that his faith, partnered with prayer, would bust down the doors.

John Maxwell, pastor, author, and leadership guru, states this about courage, *"We must focus on prayer as the main thrust to accomplish God's will and purpose on earth. The forces against us have never been greater, and this is the only way we can release God's power to become victorious."*

Look Up: I Kings 18:25-29

"Elijah said to the prophets of Baal, 'Choose one of the bulls and prepare

it first, since there are so many of you. Call on the name of your god, but do not light the fire.' So they took the bull given them and prepared it.

"Then they called on the name of Baal from morning till noon. 'Baal, answer us!' they shouted. But there was no response; no one answered. And they danced around the altar they had made.

"At noon Elijah began to taunt them. 'Shout louder!' he said. 'Surely he is a god! Perhaps he is deep in thought, or busy, or traveling. Maybe he is sleeping and must be awakened.' So they shouted louder and slashed themselves with swords and spears, as was their custom, until their blood flowed. Midday passed, and they continued their frantic prophesying until the time for the evening sacrifice. But there was no response, no one answered, no one paid attention."

The crowd was frantic. They had been pushing their agenda. Their leader had forced people to follow her ways, while her husband sat on the sidelines and went along with it. When they had to prove their position, they could not.

Look Up: I Kings 18:30-35

"Then Elijah said to all the people, 'Come here to me.' They came to him, and he repaired the altar of the Lord, which had been torn down. Elijah took twelve stones, one for each of the tribes descended from Jacob, to whom the word of the Lord had come, saying, 'Your name shall be Israel.' With the stones he built an altar in the name of the Lord, and he dug a trench around it large enough to hold two seahs of seed (about 5.75 gallons). He arranged the wood, cut the bull into pieces and laid it on the wood. Then he said to them, 'Fill four large jars with water and pour it on the offering and on the wood.'

'Do it again,' he said, and they did it again.

'Do it a third time,' he ordered, and they did it the third time. The water ran down around the altar and even filled the trench."

The people obeyed Elijah's orders. He told the prophets to water down the wood three times so there was no chance that they could question that the real God was at work.

Look Up: I Kings 18: 36-39
"At the time of sacrifice, the prophet Elijah stepped forward and prayed: 'Lord, the God of Abraham, Isaac and Israel (Jacob), let it be known today that you are God in Israel and that I am your servant and have done all these things at your command. Answer me, Lord, answer me, so these people will know that you, Lord, are God, and that you are turning their hearts back again.'

"Then the fire of the Lord fell and burned up the sacrifice, the wood, the stones and the soil, and also licked up the water in the trench.

"When all the people saw this, they fell prostrate and cried, 'The Lord—He is God!'"

The flames were so hot that they literally burned up everything—the wood, stones, soil and water. There was no doubt who was right and who was wrong.

But sometimes the lines that are drawn aren't as easy. We are afraid of what people will think or say. We're scared of how they will respond to us and how it will affect our social status.

Over the years, I've thought about my friend Sherrie, and watched her grow up. Once I left that school setting, I realized that nothing those teens said or thought was relevant, important, or long-lasting.

As a matter of fact, I had a follow-up call one day with Sherrie several years ago. When I checked in on her, I began to talk about the past. Sherrie told me about some of the terrible tragedies that had happened to her throughout her life. But she also told me about the hard things that happened while kids at school were bullying her. I felt embarrassed in those moments while we spoke. Why had I ever questioned my choice to befriend her?

Sure, the bullying feels awkward, the harassment feels bad, and the shoving and pushing seem frightening. But in the long run, are you true to God and yourself? Or are you being swayed by a side that is breaking people down? Are you changing important core values, and affecting other people negatively?

Elijah proved that God was real to the people who had at one time worshiped Baal. The God of Abraham, Isaac and Jacob was and is the only real God.

God wants our hearts, our souls, and our minds. Scripture states in Mark 12:30-31, *"Love the Lord your God with all your heart and with all your soul and with all your mind and with all your strength. The second is this: Love your neighbor as yourself. There is no commandment greater than these."* He doesn't want peer-pressured, fearful, turn-about decision makers.

For Elijah it wasn't only about loving God and loving people. It was also about being obedient to push past the voices of pressure, focus on what God said and His call, and bust down the door of fear of social pressures.

FOUR STEPS TO BUST DOWN DOORS:
These steps will encourage and remind us of the power and strength we have through the Holy Spirit to not only face the obstacles of peer pressure but to bust down the doors.

STEP ONE: *Remember* **your value and worth in Christ.**
When we are facing obstacles in front of a door that is filled with fear, bullying, and peer pressure, we know we can find strength and comfort in who we are in Christ.

> **John 1:12,** *"Yet to all who received Him, to those who believed in His name, He gave the right to become children of God."*

> **Philippians 4:13,** *"I can do all this through Him who gives me strength."*

> **II Timothy 1:7,** *"For the Spirit God gave us does not make us timid, but gives us power, love and self-discipline."*

STEP TWO: *Review* **content, truth and motivations.**
Look at what it is you're being pressured to believe and follow. Ask yourself if it is in line with your Christian faith. Question whether or not it portrays Christ-like values. Then, consider why others put pressure on people to follow them and their ideas.

> **Galatians 1:10,** *"Am I now trying to win the approval of human beings, or of God? Or am I trying to please people? If I were still trying to please people, I would not be a servant of Christ."*

> **I Thessalonians 2:4,** *"On the contrary, we speak as those approved by God to be entrusted with the gospel. We are not trying to please people but God, who tests our hearts."*

> **James 1:19-20,** *"My dear brothers and sisters, take note of this: Everyone should be quick to listen, slow to speak and slow to become angry, because human anger does not produce the righteousness that God desires."*

STEP THREE: *Resist* **anything that is against God's moral compass**

and direction.

When we're being pushed to follow the crowd and the crowd isn't following God, we need to push past fear and walk away.

> **Luke 10:19,** *"I have given you authority to trample on snakes and scorpions and to overcome all the power of the enemy; nothing will harm you."*

> **James 4:7,** *"Submit yourselves, then, to God. Resist the devil, and he will flee from you."*

> **I Peter 5:8-9,** *"Be alert and of sober mind. Your enemy the devil prowls around like a roaring lion looking for someone to devour. Resist him, standing firm in the faith, because you know that the family of believers throughout the world is undergoing the same kind of sufferings."*

STEP FOUR: *Resolve* **to be strong in your commitment to God and your faith.**

Do not bully others and respond quickly and consistently to stop bullying behavior. Once you are strong in commitment and faith, you will be able to bust down the door of your future.

> **Isaiah 35:4,** *"Say to those with fearful hearts, 'Be strong, do not fear; your God will come, He will come with vengeance; with divine retribution He will come to save you.'"*

> **Mark 12:30,** *"Love the Lord your God with all your heart and with all your soul and with all your mind and with all your strength."*

> **Ephesians 6:10-11,** *"Finally, be strong in the Lord and in His mighty power. Put on the full armor of God, so that you can take your stand against the devil's schemes."*

Throughout Scripture, we are reminded of people who **gave in** to peer pressure. Not just those who were bullied in this session's story of Elijah, Ahab and Jezebel, but others as well.

> **Esther 3:8-9:** *King Xerxes* gave in to the pressure of Haman to make people worship only the king.

> **Matthew 27:24:** *Pontius Pilate* gave in to the pressure of the crowds to crucify Christ.

> **Luke 22: 54-62:** *Peter* gave in to the pressure of the crowds to deny he knew Christ.

But, just as many people gave in to the pressures of their peers, many others stood up firmly against that same kind of peer pressure!

> **Daniel 1:8:** *Daniel* stood against the pressure to have the same unhealthy diet as the rest of the kingdom.

> **Daniel 3:16-18:** *Shadrach, Meshach and Abednego* stood against pressure to worship a golden image.

> **Mark 6:17-28:** *John the Baptist* was beheaded for standing against pressure to accept sexual immorality.

There will always be people who feel strongly about what they believe. There will be people who will have a purpose and a deep desire to convince others to believe the same things that they believe. Sometimes those things are great. Sometimes those things are evil.

Our responsibility is always to weigh those thoughts, ideas, and beliefs with what the Bible says is truth. Between the conviction of the Bible and God's Spirit, we will know to follow the pressure, or to push past the obstacles. Allow God to help us bust down the door to the real calling He is leading us towards.

In this session's story of Elijah, the people gave in to peer pressure due to fear. But if they were determining whether or not to give in to that peer pressure, they wouldn't have had to look too deeply at how to decide. By the time Elijah was done with his show-and-tell lesson, everyone knew who to believe and who to follow.

When people have to pressure you, bully you, and threaten you to agree with them, it's not right. Always remember that God is with you and will help you make the right decisions at the right time. You're never alone.

Maybe it's time for you to stop listening to the wrong voices and start focusing on the Voice that's calling you to something bigger, better, and fulfilling.

Step forward. Bust a door!

Questions:

1. Elijah had just begun his life as a prophet for God, yet at this time, many of the prophets were being killed by Queen Jezebel's orders. Why do you think Elijah asked God for permission to control the rain? Why did God give Elijah the power to stop the rain?

2. Elijah wanted to make it clear that God was the only true God. What was the significance in Elijah laying out twelve stones? Why did he make the men soak down the wood?

3. Have you ever been in a position where you felt social pressure and were bullied to agree with someone else? Discuss what that felt like and how you responded.

4. Describe a time when you watched someone being bullied to go along with the crowd. How did that person react? Were you able to help the individual and stop the bully? How will you determine your steps for future situations from what you learned in today's session?

Look Up:

1. **Deuteronomy 32:4**

2. **I Samuel 2:2**

3. **Psalm 46:1**

4. **Psalm 62:2**

5. **Psalm 94:22**

6. **Isaiah 40:29**

7. **II Corinthians 4:17**

Songs:

Hymn ~ *"Rock of Ages"* (Augustus M. Toplady & Thomas Hastings)

Contemporary ~ *"10,000 Reasons"* (Matt Redman)

Closing Prayer:

Dear Jesus,

I pray today that I will be
protected under Your shelter.

I ask today that I will be
wise in Your knowledge.

I hope today that I will be
used by Your spirit.

Help me to grow strong,
and not waver in the truths of God.

Help me to be gentle at all times,
loving in all ways, and a light that shines
in the darkness.

In Jesus' Name, *Amen*.

Daniel's Door: Values & Beliefs

*"You never know how much you believe anything
until its truth or falsehood
becomes a matter of life and death to you."*

C.S. Lewis

Door Busted: In the last lesson, we learned from Elijah that our responsibility is to weigh other people's thoughts, ideas, and beliefs with what the Bible says is truth. When following God, we can determine if we follow peer pressure or push past obstacles and bust down the door to our real calling.

Galatians 5:1, *"It is for freedom that Christ has set us free. Stand firm, then, and do not let yourselves be burdened again by a yoke of slavery."*

Growing up in southwest Iowa, my least favorite years were the ones I spent attending junior high. When I am forced to remember specific moments, my mind likes to take short detours in hopes that I won't recollect anything.

But, alas, I cannot forget several of the worst of the standout moments. Although I still cringe, I try to remind myself that in those days of being uncomfortable and challenged, I learned good lessons.

The old junior high school building stood tall and proud on the main street of Clarinda. During my three years attending junior high, I walked to and from school each day about 1½ miles each way.

At age 13, I was a funny kid. I loved God. I was the music director and pianist at my church. I was involved in the youth group and taught a kids' club on Wednesday nights.

At school, I had an ongoing agreement with my locker mate, Diana Williamson. It would be acceptable for me to tape up little posters with scripture that said, "Jesus is the Way," and it would be tolerable that she kept her cigarettes in her coat pocket. We mostly stuck to the agreement, but on several occasions those old Marlboros did roll out for the school to see.

Each day at lunchtime, I read scripture on the back staircase. During sporting events, once my school chums got past the thought process that I was an odd-duck, they began to ask me to pray. I prayed for everything. I prayed for the sporting events, prayed for people before tests, and prayed before classes.

For the most part, I got along with everyone. The snobby "in crowd" gave me a stamp of approval because they were happy that I prayed for their boyfriends and coaches before games. The druggy-smoking tough kids liked me because I would pray for Diana and opted to be kind to her.

Farm kids, smart kids, and drama kids were my friends as well. I worked hard to be kind and generous to others, but there are always those who you cannot reach.

One girl in particular, Debbie, didn't like me. Debbie was from Gun Town. In the 1920s and 1930s, they called it Gun Town because of the shootouts in the area. Tough, rough and called a "hood," Debbie resisted me, ridiculed and rallied other kids against me.

I never talked to her, never sat by her, never really knew anything about her. I could just tell by the way she looked at me, whispered, or sometimes called me "preacher" as I walked by on my way to class.

One day the principal called me to the office and warned me, "Kathy, we're worried about the rumor mill. We heard that Debbie has plans to attack and hurt you. She's spreading vicious rumors about you. We tried to talk with her about it, but she denies it. I've notified your parents. Be careful."

Deep inside, I was a wimp. I was scared. No, I was terrified. I imagined myself being beaten, black eyes, broken nose, and an arm in a cast. I questioned myself about why I had to be so open with my faith. Why would I have to risk my safety just because I wanted to pray?

But my love for God and His Spirit for loving others won out. I prayed for Debbie and asked others to pray about the upcoming day of doom. A few days later, she and her very tall friend, Anne, followed me home from school.

I remember the day as though it was yesterday. I wore a peach and white dress, tan hose, and a pair of sandals. As I quickened my step, I saw out of the corner of my eye that she held a pencil in her left hand. She whispered, laughed, bent down and jabbed that pencil into my leg. She was trying to put a run in my pantyhose, but instead she just put a jab in my leg that was painful.

When I told my folks, they said it was an opportunity to let God defend me. What?! I couldn't get past why she didn't like me. I obsessed about it day after day. I never did anything to hurt her, why was she after me?

My daddy heard my questions and spoke the truth that comes from the Spirit of God, "We don't always understand why people do what they do, but most of the time, hurting people hurt people. Let God be your defender."

At school, I saw Debbie and she and her very tall friend snickered and laughed. Some of the rumors that got back to me were horrible; some were just humorous for anyone who really knew me.

One day, I felt courageous and walked directly up to her and said, "I'm praying for you. Not sure why you don't like me, but I'm in your corner and I'm praying for you." She laughed hysterically, but oddly enough, she never tried to hurt me again. The rumors died down and Debbie set her sights on someone else.

Two years passed by and in our freshman year Debbie became pregnant. She came to school one day crying, pushing past the people to get to me. "I need to talk with you," she cried as she brushed away tears.

"Sure, what' wrong?" I asked.

"I need you to pray for me now," she whispered. I embraced her, told her I would, and asked how I could help. She stammered out the words, "I'm sorry ..." and walked away.

After nine months had passed, I saw Debbie one more time. She came to school with her baby. She told me her mother had died, her father paid no attention to her and she was so alone. Now, with her baby, she felt valuable.

I prayed with her that day, but I never saw Debbie again. That was over 40 years ago. But I remember this, God was in charge. People saw how she treated me. People saw how I treated her, and in the end, God received the glory.

Scripture tells us in Romans 12:2, *"Do not conform to the pattern of this world, but be transformed by the renewing of your mind. Then you will be able to test and approve what God's will is—His good, pleasing and perfect will."*

There will be times in our lives when we see a door of opportunity, but it is blocked by the obstacles of your fear of bodily harm. You don't want to stand up for your beliefs, for your inner core values, because you're afraid of the consequences. Behind the door remains wonderful opportunities that could provide fulfillment and satisfaction, even spiritual growth, but you just can't do it. You can't move past the looming fear of a risk that you might have to truly stand up and stand out for what you believe.

I heard of a pastor and two Christ-followers who went to a local Perkins restaurant for breakfast. One, an American veteran, sat down proudly wearing his "Make America Great Again" hat. The others, just dressed in normal attire, opened their menus and prepared to order.

But they weren't allowed to order. They were told that because of the hat, they were not welcome in the establishment. Several bullies huddled around to moan out a few bullish threats. The friends got up and left the restaurant, all the while, the vet wondered where those men and the young waiter had been while he was out dodging bullets for them and our country. Obviously, they sat safely behind the walls of Perkins, munching on toast and eggs.

If you want to stand up for what you believe, be ready to be at risk for an attack, and not just a verbal one. Be ready to face the consequences, whatever they may be. Society has openly become accepting and even valuing bullies who are physically attacking others to perpetuate their own values, opinions and agendas. Because when push comes to shove, others might be pushing and shoving you.

John F. Kennedy once said, *"Let us go forth to lead the land we love, asking His blessing and His help, but knowing that here on earth God's work must truly be our own."*

If God's work is truly our own, we need to know what we stand for, why we stand for it, and what would make us not want to stand for it any longer. Only you can choose to stand for what you truly believe, and only you can truly determine how deep your commitment lies.

Moral courage about our values and beliefs. Yes, it's a great concept, but are we willing to be strong and courageous against those who might bully us, threaten us, or physically harm us? Are we really free to express our thoughts, opinions and choices when we don't agree with others? Are we scared that if we take a stand, we might face rumors, accusations, or threats?

If we have the daily fortitude to deepen our beliefs through prayer and studying God's Word, we can build spiritual muscles that will stand fast when obstacles are blocking us from moving ahead. If we are not only strong in the knowledge of what we believe and why we believe it, we can create daily habits that continue to strengthen and deepen that faith. Those habits, in the long run, will become the ultimate strength to help bust down any doors of fear.

> Only you can choose to stand for what you truly believe, and only you can truly determine how deep your commitment lies.
>
>

As days are becoming darker and society is less accepting of Christ-followers' viewpoints and Godly morals set out for us in Scripture, we might believe that this is a problem for us today. But as we study the Bible, we see that history repeats itself over and over, such as in the story of Daniel and the lion's den.

Let's begin with one important fact. Daniel was no wimp. He was also no stranger to procuring a strong backbone when it came to what he valued and what he believed. He knew he was a child of God. He was proud of that and he did not back down. I doubt he was ever concerned about black eyes, broken bones, or very tall bullies. Instead he remained stable, strong, and secure. Without apprehension Daniel faced his door.

In Scripture, the name Daniel comes from the Hebrew name לאָיֵנָד (Daniyyel). It means *"God is my judge."* Theologians believe that Daniel was a descendant from a noble family in Judah. He was probably born in Jerusalem during the reign of Josiah.

In 597 BC, the Babylonian King Nebuchadnezzar arrived at Jerusalem determined to punish the king for refusing to pay Babylon's imposed taxes. The 18-year-old, King Jehoiachin, surrendered.

Nebuchadnezzar looted the palace and temple and took *(according to II Kings 24:14)* Jerusalem captive. He exiled the commanders and the best of the soldiers, craftsmen and artisans *(10,000 in all)*. The king ordered his officers to select the best from Judah's nobility to serve his own palace. Who is part of Judah's nobility later in scripture? Jesus!

Daniel was taken hostage, no doubt because of his noble heritage. He was treated royally because the Babylonian *(this is Iraq today)* society only sequestered the best people from a conquered land with the intent of using them to improve the overall structure and status of their society.

King Nebuchadnezzar took Daniel and three other nobles *(Shadrach, Meshach and Abednego)* prisoner, along with some of the vessels from the holy Temple to his home, Babylon. They were forced to serve the king.

As he began to serve the king as wise counsel, Daniel also interpreted several dreams for Nebuchadnezzar and became a well-respected leader.

When Babylon fell to Persian invaders in 539 BC, the new ruler, Darius the Mede, took over and promoted Daniel to Prime Minister of the

State. During this story, theologians say that Daniel was about 80 years old.

Even with his life set up to be smooth and successful for Daniel as a respected leader, life was filled with trouble. Daniel would soon be under the scrutiny of others and it would become dangerous for him.

Look Up: Daniel 6:1-4

"It pleased Darius to appoint 120 satraps (governors or rulers) *to rule throughout the kingdom, with three administrators over them, one of whom was Daniel. The satraps were made accountable to them so that the king might not suffer loss.*

"Now Daniel so distinguished himself among the administrators and the satraps by his exceptional qualities that the king planned to set him over the whole kingdom (as a Prime Minister).

"At this, the administrators and the satraps tried to find grounds for charges against Daniel in his conduct of government affairs, but they were unable to do so. They could find no corruption in him, because he was trustworthy and neither corrupt nor negligent."

Here we see the door. It's big, it's looming in the distance, and it's the sum total of what happens when we're faced with holding fast to our values and beliefs, or caving in because we are consumed with a fear of what might happen to us.

Daniel was living his life unaware of the trouble that was brewing. He was an upright citizen. He was loyal in serving his king, his government and his community. But above all, he stood firm in who he is and what and Whom he believes in ... *the God of Abraham, Isaac and Jacob.*

Unfortunately, the people around Daniel were against him. My mother always told me that the two sins that lurk in the hearts of mankind and sneak out in most situations are jealousy and control.

In this instance, the leaders saw the respect and loyalty from King Darius given to Daniel. They didn't like it, were jealous and wanted to control the situation.

Look Up: Daniel 6:5-7

"Finally these men said, 'We will never find any basis for charges against this man Daniel unless it has something to do with the law of his God.'

"So these administrators and satraps went as a group to the king and said: 'May King Darius live forever! The royal administrators, prefects, satraps, advisers and governors have all agreed that the king should issue an edict (a law) and enforce the decree that anyone who prays to any god or human being during the next thirty days, except to you, Your Majesty, shall be thrown into the lions' den.'"

The Aramaic word for den is *pit*, implying that it was underground. This is a deep pit with a small opening so the lions can't get out and neither can the prisoner.

Look Up: Daniel 6:8-9

"'Now, Your Majesty, issue the decree and put it in writing so that it cannot be altered—in accordance with the law of the Medes and Persians, which cannot be repealed.' So King Darius put the decree in writing."

This was a bad plan. A bad plan for anyone. Once you have delivered a decree in the laws of the Medes and Persians, you can't undo it. It's the old "hold fast to what you believe, or you'll be physically wounded, or even killed" situation. You thought it was just what was happening in today's world ... but, look ... there it is in the days of Daniel!

Look Up: Daniel 6:10

"Now when Daniel learned that the decree had been published, he went

home to his upstairs room where the windows opened toward Jerusalem. Three times a day he got down on his knees and prayed, giving thanks to his God, just as he had done before."

Daniel was praying according to the example of King David set up in Psalm 55:17, *"Evening, morning and noon I cry out in distress, and he hears my voice."* Three times a day he prayed. Friends, if we can feed the body three meals a day, or more, why don't we feed the soul?

The community knew about Daniel. He faced Jerusalem when he prayed, *"just as he had done before."* He had a habit of praying and talking with God. People knew about it. Maybe they know about you because of your Godly habits.

When you're downtown, you're chatting, you're leading, you're in relationship to others and people know you pray, there's no shame. There is no guilt, just the conviction that we are called to be in community with God, in relationship with His Son and His Spirit. When Daniel was following God, the administrators and satraps were trying to trap Daniel. They knew what Daniel did, and they knew how to get to him. The threat was real.

Daniel faced the door. Believed what he believed and continued to honor God alone. Or he would have to follow the newly created law that said he must back down. But Daniel didn't back down! Daniel didn't change the course. He knew what he was doing. When we have a deep relationship with the Father through prayer, inner core strength is given to us from our relationship with God.

What does inner core strength look like in this Scriptural passage? It means not backing down. Instead, we break down the door. We have the power, the energy, the force to not deny our convictions. Daniel showed strength. He wouldn't give in to the threats, the bullying, the fear. We won't give in to what the world says, because we stand for God. We are like Daniel; we are in agreement with God.

Look Up: Daniel 6:11-13

"Then these men went as a group and found Daniel praying and asking God for help. So they went to the king and spoke to him about his royal decree: 'Did you not publish a decree that during the next thirty days anyone who prays to any god or human being except to you, Your Majesty, would be thrown into the lions' den?'

"The king answered, 'The decree stands—in accordance with the law of the Medes and Persians, which cannot be repealed.'

"Then they said to the king, 'Daniel, who is one of the exiles (or captives) *from Judah, pays no attention to you, Your Majesty, or to the decree you put in writing. He still prays three times a day.'"*

The men no longer gave Daniel the respect due to him, even though he was at the very top of the leadership ladder for the Medes and Persians. Instead, they have lowered him to *"one of the exiles from Judah."* Now, he was implicated as a captive, so it doesn't sound as impressive. He was one of those guys, an old captive.

Look Up: Daniel 6:14-17

"When the king heard this, he was greatly distressed; he was determined to rescue Daniel and made every effort until sundown to save him. Then the men went as a group to King Darius and said to him, 'Remember, Your Majesty, that according to the law of the Medes and Persians no decree or edict that the king issues can be changed.'

"So the king gave the order, and they brought Daniel and threw him into the lions' den. The king said to Daniel, 'May your God, whom you serve continually, rescue you!'

"A stone was brought and placed over the mouth of the den, and the king sealed it with his own signet ring and with the rings of his nobles, so that Daniel's situation might not be changed."

To ensure that no one came to the rescue for Daniel, the King used his royal seal so that the lid of the pit could not be opened without breaking the seal. If broken, they would know someone had tried to tamper with it and rescue Daniel.

Look Up: Daniel 6:18-23
"Then the king returned to his palace and spent the night without eating and without any entertainment being brought to him. And he could not sleep.

"At the first light of dawn, the king got up and hurried to the lions' den. When he came near the den, he called to Daniel in an anguished voice, 'Daniel, servant of the living God, has your God, whom you serve continually, been able to rescue you from the lions?'

"Daniel answered, 'May the king live forever! My God sent His angel, and He shut the mouths of the lions. They have not hurt me, because I was found innocent in His sight. Nor have I ever done any wrong before you, Your Majesty.'

"The king was overjoyed and gave orders to lift Daniel out of the den. And when Daniel was lifted from the den, no wound was found on him, because he had trusted in his God."

When faced with the fear of bodily harm, Daniel chose God. He busted down the door of his fears and faced the unknown. Daniel stood in the doorway and faced lions wrapped in a blanket of God-based security. He knew that whatever happened, God was in control. Daniel stayed strong.

When we go through difficulties, when we are faced with doors of fear and we pray and trust God for the outcome, we build up our muscles of faith. We see God answer prayers. We are in communion with God. We believe in His power, His strength, His will. Daniel did not fear the physical harm, but trusted God.

I heard a challenging true story from a pastor-friend of mine. The anti-Christian Muslim terrorist group, ISIS, captured twelve Christian men and lined them up along a sandy beach to behead them.

They asked if any of the men would like to change their mind, deny Christ and admit that Allah is the only God. *(Allah is not the Christian God, as they don't believe Jesus is the Son of God).*

Each one was given the choice and shook their head, no, they would not renege. One by one they faced the door of fear of bodily harm. One by one, they stood firm, ready to bust through that door of fear to meet God on the other side. No matter the cost. No matter the consequence.

As the henchmen drew their swords to execute them one by one, a single ISIS member stepped out from the line. He looked at the men who were to be killed. He stepped up to the leader, faced the door and said, "I believe. If these men will give their lives to the One they call Jesus, who saves us from our sins, I am standing next to them and giving my life to Jesus."

That day, thirteen men busted down the door of fear and met God on the other side at the gates of Heaven. They did it boldly and with their core muscle strength that said, "I will not renege."

John Milton, an English poet from the 1600s said, *"Death is the golden key that opens the palace of eternity."*

For you and me, our situations might not be facing the door that leads to death. Instead, it might be someone pushing you in a public restaurant, pulling you out of your car, or threatening you on social media.

Perhaps it could lead to physical harm, but it might not be as serious as death. Or perhaps, it will be. Will you and I be willing to stand up and stand out for our beliefs and values? Will we look boldly into the faces of those who curse us and God, and embrace the den of lions? Are we strong enough?

The Apostle Paul tells us this, *"What is more, I consider everything a loss because of the surpassing worth of knowing Christ Jesus my Lord, for whose sake I have lost all things. I consider them garbage, that I may gain Christ and be found in Him, not having a righteousness of my own that comes from the law, but that which is through faith in Christ—the righteousness that comes from God on the basis of faith"* (Philippians 3:8-9).

THE FOUR CHARACTER QUALITIES TO EMULATE:

STEP ONE: Mature Christ-followers are *stable.*
When threatened with bodily harm because of our beliefs, we will remain confident and have stability in our actions, thoughts, and prayers. We'll have faith in God.

> **Psalm 5:11,** *"But let all who take refuge in You be glad; let them ever sing for joy. Spread Your protection over them, that those who love Your name may rejoice in You."*

> **Psalm 118:6,** *"The Lord is with me; I will not be afraid. What can mere mortals do to me?"*

> **Matthew 16:18,** *"And I tell you that you are Peter, and on this rock I will build My church, and the gates of Hades will not overcome it."*

STEP TWO: Mature Christ-followers are *strong*.

Often in life, when faced with trouble and threats, we feel we are at our weakest. But this is the time to rely on the strength and power of God. With the Holy Spirit living inside of us, we are more than conquerors over anything that comes against us.

> **Exodus 15:2,** *"The Lord is my strength and my defense; He has become my salvation. He is my God, and I will praise Him, my Father's God, and I will exalt Him."*

> **Proverbs 18:10,** *"The name of the Lord is a fortified tower; the righteous run to it and are safe."*

> **Isaiah 54:17,** *"No weapon forged against you will prevail, and you will refute every tongue that accuses you."*

STEP THREE: Mature Christ-followers are *secure*.

The world is an ever-changing place. We never know what will happen and we can never be completely confident that we will be liked, loved, or accepted. But we can be certain of one thing. God created us, loves us, sent His Son to die for us, and His love is never-ending.

> **Deuteronomy 31:8,** *"The Lord Himself goes before you and will be with you; He will never leave you nor forsake you. Do not be afraid; do not be discouraged."*

> **Psalm 32:7-8,** *"You are my hiding place; You will protect me from trouble and surround me with songs of deliverance. I will instruct you and teach you in the way you should go; I will counsel you with My loving eye on you."*

> **John 14:27,** *"Peace I leave with you; My peace I give you. I do not give to you as the world gives. Do not let your hearts be troubled and do not be afraid."*

STEP FOUR: Mature Christ-followers are *satisfied*.

Sometimes in life we determine we want more from God. We want more money, more possessions, even more days added to our lives. But we learn that when we are stable, strong and secure in God, we feel satisfied and confident in God's will. We allow God to determine what happens to us.

> **Proverbs 19:23,** *"The fear of the Lord leads to life; then one rests content, untouched by trouble."*

> **Philippians 4:11,** *"I am not saying this because I am in need, for I have learned to be content whatever the circumstances."*

> **Matthew 5:6,** *"Blessed are those who hunger and thirst for righteousness, for they will be filled."*

Perhaps in this life you will never experience the threat of bodily harm for believing in God the Father, His Son Jesus, and the Holy Spirit. Maybe you will never be bullied, threatened, or the center of someone's evil plan. But maybe, just maybe, you might find yourself like Daniel. You might be forced to decide if you'll stand for God, or risk physical harm.

Will you have the stability, strength and security to be satisfied with what God allows? Who knows, the door might present itself and you will be forced to choose. Cave in to the enemy's bullying and threats, fear what others can do, or be the one who says, "Move out of the way ... I've got inner core strength and I'm using it to bust down a door."

Questions:

1. Have you ever been in a situation where your life was threatened? If so, relay your story.

2. When Daniel learned of the decree that stated he could not pray to God, he went home, opened the windows and prayed openly. He acted boldly for his faith. Share a time when you were bold with your faith.

3. The King was very distraught that his law would affect Daniel. Why didn't he think of that before he made the edict? Do you believe that King Darius had hoped that God would rescue Daniel?

4. Describe the emotions you have when someone is harassing you for your values and beliefs. Have you ever stood up for someone else who was being harassed? Have you, or anyone you know of, ever been at the center of someone else's bad behavior due to jealousy? Describe that situation.

Look Up:

1. **Joshua 1:9**

2. **Psalm 27:1-3**

3. **Psalm 34:4**

4. **Psalm 62:1-2**

5. **Psalm 138:3**

6. **Isaiah 12:2**

7. **Philippians 4:6**

Songs:

Hymn ~ *"The Solid Rock"* (Edward Mote and William B. Bradbury)

Contemporary ~ *"You Are My King"* (Billy J. Foote)

Closing Prayer:

Dear Jesus,

I pray today that You will help me
to be stable in my thinking.
I ask that You will help me
to remain strong in my actions.

I believe that You will fill me
with the mindset of security in You.

May my heart be satisfied with
all You give,
all You are,
and all the days
I have to love and worship You.

In Jesus' Name, *Amen.*

Door Busters

Lesson Seven

Peter's Door: Waves of Doubt

*"To deny, to believe, and to doubt absolutely —
this is for man what running is for a horse."*

Blaise Pascal

Door Busted: In our last lesson, we learned from Daniel that we need to be confident in what we believe and why we believe. When we are challenged, we will be able to stay strong in that belief. Within our lifetime, opportunities may arise where we are threatened for our beliefs. Will we be able to endure and remain steadfast?

Psalm 118:5, *"Out of my distress I called on the Lord; the Lord answered me and set me free"* (ESV).

My husband's family owns a cabin up north. It's nothing spectacular or fancy, just a simple little structure that sits high up on a grassy hill overlooking a lovely lake. From the wrap-around deck, you can relax and nestle into a comfy chair, sip your tea, all the while busy little hummingbirds flit about you, sipping nectar while jetting to and fro.

Since I have been married, I've made my way from the deck at the top of the hill, down 97 wooden steps to the glorious deep blue-green waters of Lake Vermont. The trek down is never really difficult; you just have to make sure you go slow enough so as not to lose your balance and fall.

I've been out on the lake when it was calm and peaceful, like a big clear pane of glass. I've breathed in clean, crisp air, while I've watched the cows chew cud across the way. I've gazed at the turtles sunbathing in the warm light of a summer's day. And I've relaxed and enjoyed the very essence of the moment, feeling happy, contented and overly confident with life as a whole.

And then there was the day I was out on the lake with my family as we panicked when the gas gauge was misread. We ended up stranded in the middle of the lake for hours, wondering how we'd ever reach home. We never felt quite confident with that fuel indicator again.

On another occasion, I was out on the boat when a sudden rainstorm moved in and the boat rocked back and forth, waves pushed us side to side, while my heart pumped a little harder ... a little faster. I began to doubt how great life really was and lost all confidence in our ability to boat on the lake. Faith and doubt can be like that. A toss here, a smooth ride there.

One sunny bright summer day, I watched as my nephew Derek, who has cerebral palsy, rode behind the boat, happily inside a large inner tube. It was bright yellow, sunny, and happy looking. I said to myself *(who knows what I was thinking)*, "I want to do that." Momentarily insane, I told my husband, Farmer Dean, that I would like to attempt it. He was thrilled. "Face your fears!" he shouted. And so, I did.

I moved down the 97 steps to the water and climbed into the yellow inner tube. The whole time I said to myself, "Quit doubting you can do this. You can. Push past the fears."

As I stepped into the tube, I sank way down into the center of it. I sat down and hung my legs over the side. The sun was shining warm on my face, I felt confident, relaxed, at peace ... and off we went.

All of that confidence vanished within sixty short seconds.

Bump, twist, turn, punch, bump. I thought, "I'm going to die. No, first I'm going to throw up, then I'll die. I can't do this."

And sure enough, I put my hand up to signal to go slower, only to my horror, the farmer thought I meant go faster.

The faster we went, the more I saw my life fly before me like the open window that Dorothy Gale saw in *The Wizard of Oz.* As I pictured the Wicked Witch of the West riding her bike or broom, the tube flew up and flipped over with me.

Horror of horrors, terror crept up my spine. And then it hit me. This was the moment. The moment when your entire world flashes in front of you. When you realize that the Lake of Life is bigger than you are.

I saw my children, I saw my mother, I saw my laundry. Shoot ... I never got that done.

It quickly dawned on me that I couldn't get the inner tube off of my head. It had flipped over, and I was suffocating. I could hear Farmer Dean exclaiming, "You're okay! You're okay!"

Sure, I thought. He swims like a fish. I don't swim at all. His words made me mad. Mad enough to manage to make one big push to throw the inner tube off me. I gulped in a deep breath of air, coughed, choked and thought, "Now I'm going to die!"

I thought, "I'll cross myself *(I'm a Baptist so I really didn't know how to do that)* and tell God I'm ready to go." But as I put my hands to my chest, I realized I wouldn't be drowning that day. *I had forgotten I was wearing my life jacket.*

Once back inside the boat, I questioned myself. Where did the confidence I had at the beginning of my journey go? How did it disappear within my own soul? Once my eyes were cast off God and my captain, Farmer Dean, and focused on myself and all I could not do, I began to sink. Literally.

This is what life is like. Similar to a lake. When it is calm and peaceful, we have faith-filled moments and have the confidence to stand in the boat. And there are doubt-filled times when we stand up, rock the boat and lose our balance.

The only way we can bust through any doors of opportunity that are shrouded by a cloak of our own doubt and apprehension is to refocus. Stop worrying about the moments we feel we're moving too fast to a place we don't know and can't determine. We must transform our thinking and embrace the One who is calling us to Him from the doorway.

What if we stopped fearing that we can't do anything without falling and started depending on the One who can do everything without failing? What if we approached the doors of opportunity in our lives solely, whole heartedly, completely 100% dependent on the God who knows us, loves us, sees us, and is with us?

Sometimes the doubts in our hearts and minds come from living everyday life. We have trials and troubles in our marriages, our jobs, or with our families and friends. The number one issue in marriages and families today is finances.

Often, we can find ourselves in the middle of life and the next wave is coming up so high it's going to drag us under.

Pastor Charles Spurgeon once said, *"Doubt discovers difficulties which it never solves; it creates hesitancy, despondency, despair. Its progress is the decay of comfort, the death of peace. 'Believe!' is the word which speaks life into a man, but doubt nails down his coffin.*"

Scripture shows us the fear and doubts that the disciples felt when they were out on the lake in Matthew 14:22-33. The story is told in the books of Mark and John as well.

> What if we stopped fearing that we can't do anything without falling and started depending on the One who can do everything without failing?

Jesus and His disciples were out healing the sick, casting out demons, and doing great work for the Kingdom of God. Jesus had just finished performing the miracle of feeding 5,000 men, women and children. The disciples and Jesus were plain tired out. Jesus sent them out in the boat to cross the Sea of Galilee *(the Sea of Galilee is a freshwater lake in Israel whose main source is the Jordan River)* and He would meet them later.

Look Up: Matthew 14:22-24

"*Immediately Jesus made* (the Greek word here means 'to compel') *the disciples get into the boat and go on ahead of Him to the other side, while He dismissed the crowd.*"

Jesus and the disciples were headed to Bethsaida, which theologians believe adjoined the city of Capernaum (like a suburb of the larger city). John said that they are headed in the direction of Capernaum, a trading hub and fishing village, where nearly half of Jesus' disciples lived—Peter and Andrew *(fishermen brothers)*, James and John *(fishermen brothers)* and Matthew *(tax collector)*. The village was on Galilee's eastern border on a branch of the main trade route called the Way of the Sea.

"*After He had dismissed them, He went up on a mountainside by Himself to pray.*"

Jesus was discouraged as He had received the news that John the Baptist had been beheaded by Herod.

"Later that night, He was there alone, and the boat was already a considerable distance from land, buffeted by the waves because the wind was against it".

The Greek word that is translated for the word "buffeted by the waves" means "tortured or tormented." The boat was being whipped about.

John's version of the story tells us that the disciples were three miles out from the shoreline.

Look Up: John 6:19
"When they had rowed about three or four miles, they saw Jesus approaching the boat, walking on the water; and they were frightened."

Mark's rendition says that Jesus was close enough that He could see them.

Look Up: Mark 6:48a
"He saw the disciples straining at the oars, because the wind was against them."

Look Up: Matthew 14:25-26
"Shortly before dawn (between 3-6 a.m.) *Jesus went out to them, walking on the lake. When the disciples saw Him walking on the lake, they were terrified. 'It's a ghost,' they said, and cried out in fear."*

The disciples were not expecting a supernatural event out on the lake that morning. They knew that there was something different about Jesus, because they'd been eyewitnesses to many healings and miracles. However, this was different. Who is this man who defies nature itself? How could it possibly be a human being?

Look Up: Matthew 14:27

"But Jesus immediately said to them: 'Take courage! It is I. Don't be afraid.'"

Peter was faced with his first doubt. Could it possibly be Christ Himself? Why didn't Peter and the disciples recognize Jesus? They weren't looking for Jesus. Their eyes were focused on everything around them. The worries, the fretting, the fear, the trial, all overtook them. It never dawned on them to say, "Where's Jesus? We need Him now."

I have found myself in their place many times throughout my life. I see a door of opportunity, but I begin to doubt myself. I begin to look at how big the circumstances are to obtain what's behind the door. I can't think big enough, so in my own little rowboat on the Lake of Life, I have thrust the oars into the water and I'm sitting in my dark dismal surroundings doubting there is a way out. I never think to look for the Savior. Where's Jesus? I need Him now.

Warren W. Wiersbe says, *"Fear and faith cannot live in the same heart, for fear always blinds the eyes to the presence of the Lord."*

But Peter believed the voice of Jesus that said it's me, don't be scared, I'm right here with you all.

Look Up: Matthew 14:28

"'Lord, if it's You,' Peter replied, 'tell me to come to You on the water.'"

And there his opportunity began. Peter heard Jesus calling to him. The opportunity was unique, it was challenging, let's face it ... it was impossible. Whatever was behind door number one, he might not be able to get there, unless he cast everything at the foot of the One standing on water in front of him.

Look Up: Matthew 14:29

"'Come,' He said. Then Peter got down out of the boat, walked on the water and came toward Jesus."

In the moments of facing the door of opportunity and pressing your shoulder up hard against the doubts, or in this instance with Peter, your foot pushes down firmly through the door of doubt, we see faith. It's not bold and bodacious. It's not flowing freely and effervescent. It's ever so slight, ever so calm, ever so gentle. But it's recognizable. Peter was the one disciple who had enough faith and desire to answer the opportunity at the door of Christ.

Come on, Peter, I gotcha, Jesus says. No fears. No thoughts. No regrets. Just walk. Walk on the water.

Within moments, the water walking had taken over and the disciple was headed straight through that door of opportunity. Head to the Savior. Hand Him your fears. See what happens next.

As Peter put his foot over the side of the boat, the wind was whipping and blowing all around him. He began to make his way to the Savior out in the middle of the lake.

Look Up: Matthew 14:30

"But when he saw the wind, he was afraid and, beginning to sink, cried out, 'Lord, save me!'"

His fear of the waves and wind took over and he began to sink. Doubt. Doubt. Down, down, down, he went, into the darkness of the early morning hours and the murky waters. He was no longer a water walker because he had taken His eyes off of the Savior ... the only One who can help us walk on this Lake of Life.

Peter was doing a great job at water walking. I can imagine the disciples were wiping the water out of their faces and staring in disbelief. Not only was the Savior walking on top of the water, but their friend Peter stepped out of the boat and walked towards the Savior. They probably asked each other in disbelief, "What's happening!?"

But in those moments of sheer and utter obedience, and supernatural behavior, Peter began to back out of the door of opportunity and desperately searched for his comforting doubts. Where did I leave those? I can't do this. What made me think I can? It's too hard; it's too scary. The wind is too powerful. And in those moments of remorse, regret, and re-thinking, Peter began to fail and fell into the water.

Look Up: Matthew 14:31
"Immediately Jesus reached out His hand and caught him. 'You of little faith,' He said, 'why did you doubt?'"

The Savior caught him. The Savior rescued him. Not when he was drowning, but Peter recognized he was sinking and humbled himself to say ... help! I often wonder if the Savior was disappointed in him. There he was ... he was doing it. Water-walking. But as soon as his eyes were off of the Savior and onto the storm, he began to sink.

How often in life is our own behavior like this? I remember when my oldest daughter, Alexis was about six years old. We had a little orange bike we had purchased for $12.00 at a garage sale. It came with matching orange training wheels. She worked and worked to learn how to ride that bike. Day after day she would ride up and down the driveway, giggling, happy, and so very proud of herself.

Until one day she announced it was time to get rid of the training wheels. She was ready to be a big girl and go without them. I remember how excited she was—wearing little purple shorts, white button up sweater, Strawberry Shortcake tennis shoes, and a bobbing ponytail.

She watched in excitement as her dad removed each training wheel and prepared her for her first attempt at riding without them.

His pep talk consisted of the words, "You can do this! Don't be scared! Just look straight ahead at me and whatever you do, don't look down."

Alexis got on the little orange bike and for a few minutes just sat there. She said over and over, "I can't do it."

We cheered her on, "Oh, but you can!" we shouted.

She started up, put her feet on the pedals and began to ride that bike without the training wheels. She went around the driveway one full circle looking at me, looking at her dad. Then it happened. She looked down at her feet. Boom. Down she went onto the cement slab.

Her dad shouted, "What happened?"

Alexis said, "I forgot about you. I remembered my feet instead."

How often in life do we forget about the One who guards our steps, who lights our path, who ushers our way? How often do we remember our own doubts and failures and place them before our trust in the One who calls us to step out of our comfort boats and onto the lake?

Evangelical Anglican Bishop, J. C. Ryle once said, *"Doubting does not prove that a man has no faith, but only that his faith is small. And even when our faith is small, the Lord is ready to help us."*

But are we ready for the help?

Look Up: Matthew 14:32-33
"And when they climbed into the boat, the wind died down. Then those who were in the boat worshiped Him, saying, 'Truly you are the Son of God.'"

Did Jesus know that the disciples were headed into a storm when He sent them to cross the lake? Of course! Yet, He was unfolding His plan to grow their spiritual minds and hearts in faith by providing an opportunity. Not just an opportunity to see that He truly was the Son of God, but an opportunity for Peter specifically, to stretch his faith beyond his waves of doubt.

Peter should be commended for getting out of the boat and answering the call. But he should also be commended for being humble enough to ask for help. He recognized that his faith was dwindling, but He believed the Savior would rescue him.

You were doing it, Peter. Why'd you have to take your eyes off of your daddy and put them on your feet? And Christ asks him that same question when he asks, "Why did you doubt?"

Does God know that He is offering you a door of opportunity that is blocked by your own human doubt? Of course! But He is challenging you and stretching your faith. He is calling out, "Come."

Opportunities arise in life that might not be a calm and peaceful still body of water. The door might open a crack to show a flood of waters that look challenging and difficult. Yet the Father is with us through all kinds of opportunities, through all kinds of bodies of water. Whether you are in calm still waters of opportunity, or rushing currents that pull you into something new, or a door that opens to a sea of newness that feels like you might drown. God meets us at the door and is with us in the opportunities.

Look Up: Isaiah 43:2a
"When you pass through the waters, I will be with you; and when you pass through the rivers, they will not sweep over you."

God sends the call through His Son, Jesus. The waters might look too wild for any thoughts of being successful. But God is with us, through every storm, every trial, and every opportunity.

Jesus and the disciples landed their boat at Gennesaret, near Capernaum and Bethsaida. There, Jesus continued His work, once again healing the sick and preaching the truth that He was the Messiah.

Did the people know that the Savior was just out walking on the lake? Did they know that there was a storm and Jesus was in charge of the wind and the waves? After all, scripture says, *"And when they climbed into the boat, the wind died down."* Probably not. But the importance of this opportunity wasn't simply the water walking, or the faith stretching. It was also the fact that the disciples openly admitted, *"Truly you are the Son of God."*

They completely released those doubts and pushed past the door of opportunity in fully abandoning themselves to follow the Messiah, the King of Kings and Lord of Lords, the Savior, Jesus Christ. Each man in that boat pushed past their doubts that early morning and concluded that the opportunity to follow the Son of God was the opportunity of a lifetime. Their lives were transformed simply by pushing past the doubts at the doorway.

There have been so many days throughout my life where I have faced a door of opportunity and known that nothing else stood between me and that opportunity except me and my own doubts. Can I do it? Should I do it? What if I'm not good enough? What if people think I'm crazy?"

The door recently stood in front of me. The opportunity that I had imagined for over fifty years had finally come smack dab into my vantage point and I was faced with myself and my doubts.

As a little child, I had a strong pressing desire to tell others about Jesus. At age four, I loved my pastor. I mean, I really loved him as a child looks up to adults. I wanted to be just like him. He had a passion each time he stood in front of his congregation. He would pound his fist on the pulpit, sometimes wipe a tear from his eye, but mostly, he'd emphasize our need for Jesus on a weekly basis.

I remember pressing into the side of my father on that sunny Sunday morning. I pulled on his suit coat and he leaned down to hear me whisper, "I want to do that when I grow up."

"No, Kathleen, Baptists don't let women preach," he answered.

"Well, what can I do to tell people about Jesus?" I asked.

"See that woman with the tall beehive hairdo playing the piano? You can be just like her. You can lead people in worship," he suggested. "But whatever you do, Kathleen, your job, until you leave Planet Earth, is to tell people about Jesus."

I nodded, looked at the woman with the beehive hairdo, and determined to become her.

For many years, starting at age 12, I picked the hymns and worship songs for church. In my early twenties, I obtained a job as a worship director. I held that job closely, tightly as my life's dream.

But it never left me. It never went away. That door would open a crack and I'd hear the whisper, "Don't you want to preach and teach others about salvation?"

Far outweighing the voice and the desire were the doubts. How could I do this job if so many people believed it was wrong for women to be in ministry? I had heard and understood their interpretation of Paul's declaration. I also had studied the back story of what was happening at that time and why he said what he did. Nothing took away my desire to tell others about Christ.

One day my pastor told me of his dilemma. He was to be on vacation and so was our youth pastor. That left me at the helm, and he asked me to teach on Sunday. I carefully planned, studied and prepared my talk. I gave it at both morning services. I would never be the same.

Seven years later I started my nonprofit, Best Life Ministries. I spoke for each event, as well as many opportunities that arose for me in rural America.

Each time I taught, I felt a piece of my being restored. Each time I taught, I faced the door of opportunity with a wave of doubts. Could I do it? Was I smart enough? I didn't have my seminary degree; would people trust my knowledge? On and on the doubts would take shape and lure me to them, taunting and harassing me.

I learned something from my dad all those years ago. He told me when I first started in my music career, "Kathleen, sometimes we have to fake it 'til we make it." In other words, you push past the doubts, you break down the door, and you act in faith (no matter how small) like you can do it. You keep doing it and soon enough ... you are doing it and doing it well.

That's what happened. I began to speak and the more I did it, the more I'd bust down the door of doubt. The more experience I got, the better I got. But it all started with believing in God and a little bit of me, to bust the door down.

The door was completely busted down when Bethel Church in Kerkhoven, Minnesota, called me to become their lead pastor. I had filled in for their pastor for years. They knew me, they believed in me, they trusted me. The call was there. I answered it. Fears, doubts, and everything. Just laid it right down before God and He said, "If you choose to do this, I'll help you." And He has!

Perhaps you have a door of opportunity standing in front of you today, but you're overwhelmed with yourself. You've taken your eyes off of the Savior and His power, and you've looked down at your own little feet that are off of the pedals, off of the water, and you're falling and sinking fast.

You believe the lies that the Enemy is perpetuating inside your heart and mind. He's saying you're not enough ... you can never do it ... it's too hard, too big, too much. All along you hear the voice of the Savior saying, "It's not too hard for Me, too big for Me, or too much for Me. I'll help you."

Break them down. Push them out. Cast them away to the foot of the cross. For the power is not yours, it never was. It belongs to the One who is the door. Doubts just get us tangled up and believing we need to use our training wheels forever. It's time to pitch those and get moving ... with the help of the Savior.

Dr. Caroline Leaf says this about thinking thoughts that are negative and filled with doubt, *"As we think, we change the physical nature of our brain. As we consciously direct our thinking, we can wire out toxic patterns of thinking and replace them with healthy thoughts."*

FOUR STEPS TO ENCOURAGE MOVING FORWARD:

STEP ONE: *Make* time for God.
When we pray and read scripture, we develop a strong relationship with God. We look to Him for who we are and determine that we can do whatever He calls us to do, through His power.

Psalm 1:2, *"But whose delight is in the law of the Lord, and who meditates on His law day and night."*

Matthew 6:33, *"But seek first His kingdom and His righteousness, and all these things will be given to you as well."*

Philippians 4:13, *"I can do all this through Him who gives me strength."*

STEP TWO: *Manage* your thinking.

When we let our thoughts and emotions take over, we can end up with negative thinking, a bad attitude, and a wave of doubt. If we take our thoughts captive to God and replace negative "I can't" with positive "I can with You, God," we are able to bust down doors of doubt.

Romans 12:2, *"Do not conform to the pattern of this world, but be transformed by the renewing of your mind. Then you will be able to test and approve what God's will is—His good, pleasing and perfect will."*

II Corinthians 10:5, *"We demolish arguments and every pretension that sets itself up against the knowledge of God, and we take captive every thought to make it obedient to Christ."*

Philippians 4:8, *"Finally, brothers and sisters, whatever is true, whatever is noble, whatever is right, whatever is pure, whatever is lovely, whatever is admirable—if anything is excellent or praiseworthy—think about such things."*

STEP THREE: *Motivate* yourself through God's eyes.

When we look at all of the scriptures that tell us how God sees us, we can be encouraged! We are loved, cherished, created, and have a purpose. When we believe the good things that the Father says about us, this helps cast off doubts in our abilities. When we rely on Him, we have His power to do whatever He calls us to do.

John 1:12, *"Yet to all who received Him, to those who believed in His name, He gave the right to become children of God."*

Romans 8:1, *"Therefore, there is now no condemnation for those who are in Christ Jesus."*

Colossians 2:9-10, *"For in Christ all the fullness of the Deity lives in bodily form, and you have been given fullness in Christ, who is the head over every power and authority."*

STEP FOUR: *Maintain* **your heart.**

Once you build a strong relationship with God, you develop a healthier way to look at yourself. But it's important to not allow sin to build up. Recognize it and confess it. Having doubts in yourself is normal, believing that you are incapable and unable to answer God's calls. Doubts can be an easy way to become disobedient.

> **Deuteronomy 11:1,** *"Love the Lord your God and keep His requirements, His decrees, His laws and His commands always."*

> **John 15:14,** *"You are my friends if you do what I command."*

> **II John 1:6,** *"And this is love: that we walk in obedience to His commands. As you have heard from the beginning, His command is that you walk in love."*

Maybe you are standing in front of a wonderful door of opportunity. Unfortunately for you, the doubts that you have about your own abilities, the outcome, and even the opportunity itself have completely clouded your viewpoint. You can't see anything except the big looming wave of doubts.

But maybe the door is open a crack and you can hear the rushing waters of change making its way through the fog of doubt. You hear the call, you know it's something great, doubt and uncertainty disappear.

It's time to take a step. It's time to take 97 steps right down to your yellow inner tube. Take that chance, grab that door handle, push it until it opens and take that first step. It might seem like the water is a little bumpy, but you'll never know unless you step out in faith.

Questions:

1. Have you ever passed up a great opportunity because you had too many doubts about the outcome? If so, share that situation.

2. Peter asked, Lord, if it's You, tell me to come to You on the water. Why did Peter question who He was and why did he want Jesus to call to him?

3. The disciples had witnessed miraculous healings and even Jesus feeding the 5,000 and still didn't believe. Why does Scripture say after they saw Him on the water, *"Then those who were in the boat worshiped Him, saying, 'Truly You are the Son of God.'"*? What was the difference between other miracles and this incident?

4. Name a specific door of opportunity that you have right now but are doubting your own abilities. After this lesson, what will you do to change your attitude, face the waves of doubt and bust through the door?

Look Up:

1. **II Samuel 22:33**

2. **I Chronicles 16:11**

3. **Nehemiah 8:10**

4. **Psalm 46:1-3**

5. **Isaiah 26:3-4**

6. **John 6:16-21**

7. **Romans 15:13**

Songs:

Hymn ~ *"Turn Your Eyes Upon Jesus"* (Helen H. Lemmel)

Contemporary ~ *"Cornerstone"* (Mote, Liljero, Myrin, Morgan, Bradbury)

Closing Prayer:

Dear Jesus,

I confess my inability to do
anything without Your power.

I am afraid. I have my doubts.
I feel unsure in my own abilities.

Help me to keep my eyes fixed on You
and help me to believe in Your power.

In Jesus' Name, *Amen.*

Paul's Door: Discouragement

*"God puts dreams in your heart that are bigger than you
so that you will rely on Him and His power."*

Tony Evans

Door Busted: In the last lesson, we learned from Peter that each one of us will experience moments in life where we question ourselves and wonder if we could possibly do what God is asking of us. These are the moments where we put our faith in Him, keep our eyes on Him, and look to Him for success and fulfillment. Any other way just won't work.

Psalm 28:7, *"The Lord is my strength and my shield; my heart trusts in Him, and He helps me."*

The day was a beautiful fall afternoon. The hues of yellows, reds, and browns cast lovely reflections off of the trees onto the lush grass. As far as your eye could see, fall was stretched out on the grounds before us.

Our church had advertised a fun-filled Sunday afternoon get-together that included various musical selections, speakers, and lots of encouragement. As assistant to the music director, I nervously paced back and forth going over every detail with him to make sure the event would be a big success.

Earlier that week at the planning meeting where we would review the details, our lead pastor was in a jovial mood. That typically meant one end result ... being teased. He loved to poke fun at the staff and find where they had hidden their hopes and dreams. He'd pull them out and try to spoof them. I'm not sure I ever really understood his tactics or even his motivation, but I did everything to make sure I didn't get into the spotlight. Until that week.

Somehow the pastor had found out my deepest heartfelt desire. The door of opportunity that had called to me over and over was simple. I wanted to sing commercials for the radio.

The call began when I was about age twelve. I would watch our old black and white television set at night after all my homework was completed. I'd desperately wait through the television shows until the commercials arrived, and there, within those thirty-second jingles, I would find my heart's delight. Commercials.

I know it was a strange obsession, but it was mine, and so I learned the catchy little tunes that accompanied products. Songs like "Two hundred million people, no two are quite the same ..." from Burger King, or "I wish I were an Oscar Meyer wiener ..."

Throughout the years, above any and all jingles, my favorite commercial was for Folgers coffee. I sang it at school, I sang it at work, I sang it on bike rides, I sang it when I had my children. My hopes and dreams were that someday I would sing for the Folgers company.

My pastor found out about this desire and began to make fun of it. It was discouraging, disappointing and humiliating. Everyone at the table laughed at his attempt of acting like me singing a Folgers' commercial.

"Sing it, Kathy ... sing it," he taunted. So, I did. I stood up and boldly sang it while the others burst into fits of laughter.

"What a huge dream," my worship director-boss stated. "Kind of unreal, don't you think?"

Discouragement began to settle in.

"Singing commercials! Ha. That's ridiculous. You work here at the church. It'd never happen to someone like you," the pastor said as he walked away.

But here's the wonderful thing about God. He never gives us dreams just to give us dreams. He never calls us from behind the door to taunt or tease us. He has a plan and a purpose. Scripture tells us in Psalm 37:4, *"Take delight in the Lord, and He will give you the desires of your heart."*

Although I felt embarrassed, I moved on towards the big Sunday event. Now that it was unfolding, I felt relieved as song after song was performed. People milled about with a contented attitude and seemed to be enjoying the lovely fall day.

And then it happened. The pastor stood up to continue his job of emceeing and began to taunt me in front of the crowd of 500 people. I felt my face getting hot and begged God for the earth to open up and swallow me whole.

"Come on up here, Kathy," he teased. "You see Kathy's got this dream. She wants to *(insert his laughter)* sing the jingle for Folgers. Sing it, Kathy! Sing it!"

The crowd began to clap and chant, "Folgers ... Folgers."

I grabbed the microphone and closed my eyes just as I had done when I was ten years old and held my hairbrush in front of the bathroom mirror while singing. I sang out and I sang proud, "The day's lookin' new and bright, and you're gonna start it right, Folgers startin' to brew, the aromas callin' you. The best part of wakin' up, is Folgers in your cup."

The crowd jumped to their feet cheering and clapping. I took a bow, waved and blew kisses and crept off the stage. Although I made light of it, I felt hurt. How was it so easy for others to make fun of the door and the call?

Although several people stopped to say great job, most people discouraged me from such a lofty dream. No one ever walks in to the doorway of singing jingles.

I made my way to the back of the crowd where the food stands were set up. I asked for a diet Pepsi *(not a cup of coffee!)* and tried to hide out of view. I breathed this prayer: *"God, I believe in this crazy talent, this love for jingles. I think You put it in my heart and mind back when I was ten. It doesn't matter if people believe in me or not because I think You believe in me. So, I'll keep singing jingles in front of the mirror, and I won't be afraid or take on the discouragement and harassment of others. I kick that attitude off and I take on my faith in You. Amen."*

I opened my eyes and much to my surprise, a young man of about thirty was making his way toward me. He walked up, held out his hand and gave me a business card. He said, "Kathy, my name is Joel. I'm a jingle producer here in the Twin Cities. Your Folgers commercial was great. Call me tomorrow and let's get you in the studio for a demo test. I think you could have a great future in singing jingles."

Right as he began talking, my boss, the worship director, came up to us. He heard the whole conversation and his mouth dropped wide open. We both were shocked. Not only was I elated, but when the discouragement was cast off, God allowed me to bust through that door.

The door flew open and I spent the next seven years working with producers in the Twin Cities singing commercials for radio stations throughout the Midwest. When God puts a dream in our hearts and stands behind the door of opportunity, He waits to see if we'll have faith or become discouraged. It's up to us to push past it or give up.

There is nothing worse than having people stand strongly against a deep passion that you carry in the depths of your soul. I believe that when God gives us a passionate desire to do something *(a dream)* that will not dissipate after years have gone by,

> When God plants a dream in your soul, it's your job to grow and nurture that dream. In doing so, you fulfill the destiny that He chooses to grow from your life.

that dream is meant to be. It is something God has desired for you to follow. But you alone can work with God to make that dream happen. You must decide if you will work with Him even if everyone around you laughs and tells you you're an idiot.

When God plants a dream in your soul, it's your job to grow and nurture that dream. In doing so, you fulfill the destiny that He chooses to grow from your life.

Dreams are a funny thing. They make no sense to others because they are not given to others. They are given to us. It's only when we face the door, hear the call, and see the obstacle of others trying to talk us out of it, that we can know how deep the dream goes.

There have been times in my life when I have believed in a call so strongly that no one could have talked, teased, or taunted me out of it. And there have been times in my life when I have felt a call or a prompting to do something where others have easily swayed me or simply talked me out of it without much effort.

When it's a true-life call from God, no human can change your mind. The call does not go away with time and it does not go away with discouragement. It stands firm. It strengthens you with each day that goes by. But you must find your way past the people discouraging you and make your way to the One who is encouragement at its best—God.

I often wonder the purpose behind the voices that tell us we can't do something, or that we have a crazy dream. Is it because those people don't dream big themselves? Is it because they are afraid? Or are they placed there to be the impetus that tests the very core of our being? Are they allowed to be there and, in so doing, challenge us to step up to the door and determine if it is worth our time and our effort? I believe that everyone needs a cheerleader. I believe that no one should be in the position to discourage others from their dreams. No one.

Fred Rogers, the incredibly gifted host of *Mister Rogers' Neighborhood* television show for children once said, *"As human beings, our job in life is to help people realize how rare and valuable each one of us really is, that each of us has something that no one else has—or ever will have— something inside that is unique to all time. It's our job to encourage each other to discover that uniqueness and to provide ways of developing its expression."*

But what do we do when the voices of others discourage us? How do we deal with the teasing and ridicule? How do we truly know when we can muster enough courage to bust down the door?

Instead of being those who are standing in front of the door of opportunity blocking it for others, we should be encouragers, not discouragers! How wonderful it would be if we could see others being raised up, being believed in, and being propelled to a greater cause because God used our words to help them soar!

Encouragement is the language of the New Testament. The words *"to encourage"* are used more than 100 times in the New Testament.

Within the New Testament, we learn of a man who is a great example of bringing encouragement to others. His real name is Joseph.

We learn about Joseph for the first time in Acts 4.

Look Up: Acts 4:36-37
"Joseph, a Levite from Cyprus whom the apostles called Barnabas, (which means son of encouragement) sold a field he owned and brought the money and put it at the apostles' feet."

Joseph had a nickname. So well-known to those in his region, people nicknamed him Barnabas because he was filled with encouragement that he poured out to others.

In my own family, everyone has a nickname. The truth is, I love nicknames and I'd give you a nickname if I could. I nickname everyone. My son-in-law, Josh, is called Bob. My grandson, Noah, is called Gus. My daughter, Alexis, is called Alan. My middle daughter, Chandra, is called Tater. My youngest daughter, Jenessa, is called Babs.

Everyone in my circle of close friends has a nickname. I see who they are and how they act, and I connect them to that something that makes them special. At my house, Dean's nickname is Buddy, Deano and Farmer Dean. My nickname is Ma'am.

Joseph was nicknamed Barnabas—*son of encouragement.* What a fabulous nickname. Much better than Gus or Tater.

Joseph, or Barnabas, was a Levite. Levites were from one of the tribes of Israel. Levites were assigned no regional inheritance like the other tribes of Israel. Instead, they were assigned towns to live in and given pastures for their flocks and herds.

In those days, Levites served as assistants to the priests—as doorkeepers or musicians in the temple. But Barnabas couldn't own that position because he was from Cyprus, which meant he hadn't been born in Israel. Cyprus was 293 miles from Israel.

He was a Hellenist—a name given to Israelites born overseas. They were regarded as foreigners. They did not speak Aramaic like Jesus, the disciples and the Jews spoke. And they were considered to have picked up Gentile ways. Kind of the cast-offs in life.

There was a lot of hostility between native-born Israelites and the Hellenists. Because of that tension, Barnabas wasn't allowed to serve in the temple like his people the Levites would have normally been permitted.

We would expect Barnabas to be crabby and disappointed. He could have been jealous, impatient, and felt left out. But instead, Barnabas was an encourager. He saw a need and wanted to build others up. He built up the followers of Jesus and helped them by saying I own some property. I could sell some land to help out. Let me help you in your quest to share the gospel.

Barnabas is the first recorded donor in this new community of "Followers of the Way" *(Christ-followers)*. When scripture said he put the money at the apostles' feet, he was saying: You'll know what to do with it. No strings attached. Just be encouraged.

Barnabas encouraged the community, the community encouraged Barnabas. That's how encouragement works. That's how giving works. That's how not blocking the doors of opportunity for others works.

After this episode, scripture doesn't talk about Barnabas until Acts chapter nine. There, we read about a man named Saul of Tarsus *(eventually he's referred to as the Apostle Paul)* who had been killing

Christ-followers. But on the road to Damascus, Saul had a come-to-Jesus meeting. He repented and trusted Jesus. His life completely turned about from Christ-follower killer to Christ-follower period.

Look Up: Acts 9:1-4
"Meanwhile, Saul was still breathing out murderous threats against the Lord's disciples. He went to the high priest and asked him for letters to the synagogues in Damascus, so that if he found any there who belonged to the Way, whether men or women, he might take them as prisoners to Jerusalem."

Damascus was about 150 miles from Tarsus, or four to six days travel.

"As he neared Damascus on his journey, suddenly a light from heaven flashed around him. He fell to the ground and heard a voice say to him, 'Saul, Saul, why do you persecute me?'"

A wake-up call. A call to change. A call for transformation from old to new. Saul answered the call and eventually became the Apostle Paul.

Look Up: Acts 9:5-9
"'Who are you, Lord?' Saul asked.

'I am Jesus, whom you are persecuting,' he replied. 'Now get up and go into the city, and you will be told what you must do.'

"The men traveling with Saul stood there speechless; they heard the sound but did not see anyone. Saul got up from the ground, but when he opened his eyes he could see nothing. So they led him by the hand into Damascus. For three days he was blind, and did not eat or drink anything."

Here's the first call to Saul from behind the door. Just as we hear the call, we also hear the first voice of discouragement as it pronounces its unbelief.

Look Up: Acts 9:10-15
The Call for Helping Saul Reach His Destiny:

"In Damascus there was a disciple named Ananias. The Lord called to him in a vision, 'Ananias!'

'Yes, Lord,' he answered.

"The Lord told him, 'Go to the house of Judas on Straight Street and ask for a man from Tarsus named Saul, for he is praying. In a vision he has seen a man named Ananias come and place his hands on him to restore his sight."

The Discouragement:

"'Lord,' Ananias answered, 'I have heard many reports about this man and all the harm he has done to your holy people in Jerusalem. And he has come here with authority from the chief priests to arrest all who call on Your name.'"

Confirmation of his Call:

"But the Lord said to Ananias, 'Go! This man is My chosen instrument to proclaim My name to the Gentiles and their kings and to the people of Israel. I will show him how much he must suffer for My name.'"

God has reaffirmed His plan for Saul's life. God saw Ananias standing in front of Saul's door and gently pushed him aside. No discouragement needed, just affirmation for the plan.

Look Up: Acts 9:17-19

"Then Ananias went to the house and entered it. Placing his hands on Saul, he said, 'Brother Saul, the Lord—Jesus, who appeared to you on the road as you were coming here—has sent me so that you may see again and be filled with the Holy Spirit.' Immediately, something like scales fell from Saul's eyes, and he could see again. He got up and was

baptized, and after taking some food, he regained his strength."

Once he was stronger, Saul got up and got to work telling others about the salvation that Jesus Christ had given to mankind when He shed His blood at Calvary.

But when Saul got to Jerusalem, he heard that call. Once again, the same strong voice from behind the door that had said, Saul, Saul, why do you persecute me? Now, called out, Saul, Saul, serve me ... serve me.

Saul's passion drew him to Christ's disciples to partner with them in their endeavors of spreading the saving knowledge of Jesus. Instead, they stood in front of the door of the call. They didn't want anything to do with him.

Look Up: Acts 9:20-22

"Saul spent several days with the disciples in Damascus. At once he began to preach in the synagogues that Jesus is the Son of God. All those who heard him were astonished and asked, 'Isn't he the man who raised havoc in Jerusalem among those who call on this name? And hasn't he come here to take them as prisoners to the chief priests?' Yet Saul grew more and more powerful and baffled the Jews living in Damascus by proving that Jesus is the Messiah."

Baffled. Wasn't Saul a Jew? Didn't he follow the laws of Moses? Didn't he say that Jesus Christ wasn't the Messiah. They were confused and baffled by his complete turnabout.

Scripture tells us that Saul tried to join the disciples, but they were afraid of him. What if he's still killing Christ-followers? They couldn't believe the best of him. They'd only heard of his worst.

Look Up: Acts 9:26

"When he came to Jerusalem, he tried to join the disciples, but they were

all afraid of him, not believing that he really was a disciple."

The disciples developed a great idea. Let's get the encourager, Barnabas, to talk with Saul. He'll tell us the truth. He sees the best in everyone.

So, they sent Barnabas to check out Saul.

Look Up: Acts 9:27
"But Barnabas took him and brought him to the apostles. He told them how Saul on his journey had seen the Lord and that the Lord had spoken to him, and how in Damascus he had preached fearlessly in the name of Jesus. So Saul stayed with them and moved about freely in Jerusalem, speaking boldly in the name of the Lord."

He tried to join the disciples. He faced the door, saw the obstacle of discouragement, fear and disbelief from others, and he pushed past them. But God did something a little different in this situation. He used the encouragement from someone else to come in, partner with the push of Saul, and it busted down the door.

Encouragers don't limit you. They don't discourage you. They don't tell you that you can't do something. They don't stand in front of the door of opportunity. Instead they see your giftedness and they support, lift up and propel you to keep going ... keep moving ... don't stop now! Bust it down. Get through that door.

Barnabas was willing to take a risk with Saul. Barnabas became Saul's friend and saw the good in him. He saw a vision of the calling that Saul had on his life to teach about Jesus. So, he pushed, prodded, built into him, and encouraged him to move forward. Barnabas, the encourager, was inclined to see the best and call it out. He went to his brothers and said: Look at the change! Look at who he is and what he's doing now. Come on, guys, you can trust Him.

The disciples embraced Saul, because Barnabas said Saul could be trusted. Saul stayed with them in Jerusalem serving God and answering the call.

What would have happened to Saul if he had not had Barnabas? It might not have had the same end result. Instead, thanks to someone who believed in him, Paul was accepted and was propelled on to good work for God because of someone's encouragement.

You and I can do that for those around us. We can build someone up to follow their destiny.

Reverend Henry Drummond from the 1800s once said, *"What a noble gift it is, the power of playing upon the souls and wills of men, and rousing them to lofty purposes and holy deeds."*

How sad it is to think that there are some who will doubt our abilities, doubt our call, and doubt our motives. But that's life and all that it's made up of. There will be people who stand in front of us in disbelief and say, "It can't be done." Or, like I experienced with the jingles, there will be some who think your call is less than realistic or even stupid. They won't hesitate in letting you know their opinion.

How hard will you follow after God? How strong will their discouragement be in your life? Will you and I allow them to attempt to change the course set by God?

Encouragers are not jealous of others' successes. In Romans 12:15, the Apostle Paul says, *"Rejoice with those who rejoice."*

Saul and the disciples followed their call to serve God by sharing the good news of His Son, Jesus. Encouragement ran rampant throughout the land.

Look Up: Acts 9:31

"Then the church throughout Judea, Galilee and Samaria enjoyed a time of peace and was strengthened. Living in the fear of the Lord and **encouraged by the Holy Spirit,** *it increased in numbers."*

Even the Holy Spirit was about the work of encouragement!

There are days when I am depleted. I am the one who looks at the door and thinks, "I can't do it." Someone walks in and says, "I don't think you can do that either."

If you are anything like me, when we are feeling doubtful and negative, we can take on the discouragement of others.

God doesn't intend for us to let our dreams become open knowledge to every passerby. Instead, He carefully plants the seeds of dreams in our souls so that we carry those seeds, we water them, nourish them, and He produces the destiny. But it all starts with a call from the door of opportunity. He's not calling others to that door. It's meant for you alone. Why would we let others have a part in discerning our steps?

You and I are personally encouraged by the Spirit of the Living God throughout our lives. We are given steps that lead us to the moment we hear the call. It's not the job of others to discourage us if God has a plan for us. It's their job to be like Barnabas. See the truth, see the talents, see the heart, and help make that truth known.

Barnabas disappeared from scripture until another critical moment within the history of the church. The disciples counted on their positive, encouraging friend, Barnabas, to help them. Those who are encouragers are used in big ways to help bust down door-blockers for God.

Look Up: Acts 11:20-24

"Some of them, however, men from Cyprus and Cyrene, went to

Antioch and began to speak to Greeks also, telling them the good news
about the Lord Jesus. The Lord's hand was with them, and a great number
of people believed and turned to the Lord.

"News of this reached the church in Jerusalem, and they sent Barnabas
to Antioch. When he arrived and saw what the grace of God had done,
he was glad and encouraged them all to remain true to the Lord with all
their hearts. He was a good man, full of the Holy Spirit and faith, and a
great number of people were brought to the Lord."

Antioch is where the Bible first says that God opened the door of His
message of salvation to the Gentiles. It wasn't long before Barnabas
realized he was going to need somebody to help him deal with this
new opportunity—somebody who knew the Scriptures, someone who
could speak to the Gentiles and had a strong faith.

He remembered Saul. This was ironic, because no one had been more
Jewish than Saul. No one had more zeal for the Torah than Saul. But
Barnabas thought that there was something in him that could be
developed.

Remember, encouragers see the best in others and propel them to good
work. They are not the discouragement standing in the doorway.

Saul continued to do his amazing work for God and eventually in Acts
13:9 refers to himself as Paul. *"Then Saul, who was also called Paul, filled*
with the Holy Spirit ..."

Saul was the Jewish version of his name; Paul was Greek or Gentile. He
would become the great missionary to the Gentiles and the rest of the
world. Paul would change the world, but it happened because of a call,
a push past discouragers, and a partnership with an encourager.

Paul and Barnabas did ministry together, and an interesting thing happened. In the ancient world, it was significant to look at the order of people's names because that order tells you who's in charge, who's the boss, and who carries the prestige of the mission.

In Acts, we read that for an entire year Barnabas and Paul taught great numbers of people in Antioch. They sent Barnabas and Paul to deliver their gifts to the leaders in Jerusalem. Barnabas and Paul were chosen by the Holy Spirit to do special work.

But something happened in this process of time passing by. Paul's gifts began to flourish; his maturity began to blossom. He was fulfilling the answer to the door of opportunity. Acts 14 says, *"At Iconium Paul and Barnabas went to the synagogues."* Did you catch what happened there? The names have been switched. Now Paul is the one leading.

From a human standpoint, this was terrible. The mission has been a big success; Barnabas should have made sure he received the credit.

Barnabas could have been jealous, but he wasn't. He was an encourager. That-a-boy, Paul. You did it. I believed in you all along. God helped me see who you were, and you have gifts that needed to be used. I helped you push past the discouragers and bust down the door. An encourager believes, supports, propels.

When we hear the discouragement of others, when we feel the sting of their criticism and see the sarcastic attitude that takes over their countenance, we can be dissuaded from our destiny. Or we can push past that negativity and get to the Voice who knows us best, who believes in us and encourages us along.

FOUR STEPS TO ENCOURAGE MOVING PAST DISCOURAGEMENT:

STEP ONE: *Let go* of the opinions of others.

When we take on other people's thoughts and opinions of what we can and cannot do, we are dishonoring God and ourselves. We limit who we are and who we will become with God's help, because we are held down by the restricted view from others' vantage point.

> **Psalm 34:18,** *"The Lord is close to the brokenhearted and saves those who are crushed in spirit."*

> **Psalm 55:22,** *"Cast your cares on the Lord and He will sustain you; He will never let the righteous be shaken."*

> **II Corinthians 4:8-9,** *"We are hard pressed on every side, but not crushed; perplexed, but not in despair; persecuted, but not abandoned; struck down, but not destroyed."*

STEP TWO: *Look for* encouragers.

The world is always filled with those who will discourage and dissuade you, but it's also filled with people who will lift you up and believe in your abilities. Find those encouragers and journey with them by your side!

> **John 15:12,** *"My command is this: Love each other as I have loved you."*

> **I Thessalonians 5:11,** *"Therefore encourage one another and build each other up, just as in fact you are doing."*

> **Hebrews 13:16,** *"And do not forget to do good and to share with others, for with such sacrifices God is pleased."*

STEP THREE: *Listen* **to how God defines you.**

If we give in to the opinions of others who tell us that we are unworthy, unable, and incapable, we begin to believe those lies. The truth is that without God, none of us can do anything. But if He is calling you to it, He's committed to seeing you through it. Memorize how God sees you … His chosen one.

> **Romans 8:37,** "*No, in all these things we are more than conquerors through Him who loved us.*"

> **II Corinthians 5:17,** "*Therefore, if anyone is in Christ, the new creation has come: The old has gone, the new is here!*"

> **Galatians 3:26,** "*So in Christ Jesus you are all children of God through faith.*"

STEP FOUR: *Live* **your destiny.**

Each one of us is made up of unique talents and personality traits. Sometimes those who have known us intimately, or even have been a boss or a neighbor, might not see us with the same complete picture of who we truly are and who we can become. We must not let anyone's discouragement stop us from God-appointed opportunities.

> **Isaiah 46:10,** "*I make known the end from the beginning, from ancient times, what is still to come. I say, 'My purpose will stand, and I will do all that I please.'*"

> **Isaiah 55:11,** "*So is My word that goes out from My mouth: It will not return to Me empty, but will accomplish what I desire and achieve the purpose for which I sent it.*"

> **Habakkuk 2:3,** "*For the revelation awaits an appointed time; it speaks of the end and will not prove false. Though it linger, wait for it; it will certainly come and will not delay.*"

Gregory of Nyssa, a theologian from 372 A.D. who made significant contributions to creating the Nicene Creed, was one of the early church fathers in the fourth century. He painted a beautiful picture of a way of living that would encourage others. He wrote: *"At horse races, the spectators intent on victory shout to their favorites in the contest. From the balcony they incite the rider to keener effort, urging the horses on while leaning forward and flailing the air with their outstretched hand instead of a whip."*

With that visual picture created in our minds, he went on to say: *"I seem to be doing the same thing myself, most valued friend and brother. While you are competing admirably in a divine race, straining constantly for the prize of the heavenly calling, I exhort, urge and encourage you vigorously."*

The Apostle Paul stood at the door of opportunity, and a great opportunity it was. A life filled with beatings, floggings, persecution, jail time and some time stranded on an island.

But through all of that, he wrote thirteen books of the Bible, led multitudes of people to Christ, healed the sick, and became a great leader who continues to have a huge impact on our lives today.

Instead of being struck down and absorbing the negativity, doubt, and discouragement from the other disciples, Paul listened to his newly-found-friend, Barnabas, Son of Encouragement. That friend helped bust down a door. A big door.

Let's remember that encouragement can be the strong arm of help someone needs to reach their potential. Or maybe ... bust down a big door.

Questions:

1. The disciples were afraid of Saul and didn't trust him. If you were in their shoes, discuss how you would respond to his desire to work alongside you.

2. Once Barnabas listened to Paul's vision for the opportunity God had given him, Barnabas was excited and determined to convince the disciples to partner with him. Name a time when someone positively encouraged others about you. Name a time when you positively encouraged others about someone else.

3. Do you find yourself frequently discouraging others from opportunities? If so, take a moment and talk about why you think you respond that way toward others.

4. This week, if given the chance to hear someone's dream, would you dismiss it, laugh at it, or encourage that person to follow the call? Take a moment and discuss why you would discourage or encourage them.

Look Up:

1. Proverbs 16:3

2. Proverbs 20:24

3. Jeremiah 29:11-12

4. Romans 8:28

5. Ephesians 2:8

6. I Thessalonians 5:5

7. II Thessalonians 2:16-17

Songs:

Hymn ~ *"Savior Like a Shepherd Lead Us"* (William B. Bradbury)

Contemporary ~ *"I Am Free"* (John Egan)

Closing Prayer:

Dear Jesus,

When I listen to the voices of others and
take upon myself their words of discouragement,
help me to remember that You believe in me.

Help me to focus on Your voice alone.
In a world filled with so much negativity,
help me be an encourager to others.

In Jesus' Name, *Amen.*

Lesson Nine

Deborah's Door: Oppression

*"To me, it has been a source of great comfort
and strength in the day of battle,
just to remember that the secret of steadfastness,
and indeed, of victory,
is the recognition that the Lord is at hand."*

Duncan Campbell

Door Busted: In our last lesson, we learned from Paul that other people can discourage us from the dreams and future that God has set out before us. Instead of allowing their negative talk and criticism to affect us, we need to rise above those words and attitudes. We need to believe that God is for us and with us, and He will remind us of who we truly are through His eyes.

Psalm 71:4, *"Deliver me, my God, from the hand of the wicked, from the grasp of those who are evil and cruel."*

The day was warm and bright, amidst the late summer days of June. I had taped the class reunion invitation to the refrigerator so that I would not lose it.

Earlier that week, I spent time shopping for the perfect outfit that would be appropriate for the event. It wasn't every day I would accompany my husband to his class reunion.

I wrapped up all of my meetings and rehearsals at church early that day so I could get home to dress and be ready to go.

The kids were scattered with their own lives. One at cheerleading practice, one at work, and one at a friend's house. I wasn't worried about cooking any dinner or driving children to their prospective events.

I remember how I took my time getting dressed, putting on my makeup ever so carefully, getting my hair just right, and spraying on a finishing touch of perfume. I thought to myself that my new outfit looked good and I did the best I could with how I looked.

Unfortunately for me, it wasn't good enough. Nothing was ever good enough for my spouse. I had lived with the oppression so long, that it had become the norm for me and for my girls.

I opened the screen door in search of my spouse. As I leaned out on the front step, there he was digging in the ground, planting some shrub. I said, "You better get a move on, because we'll be late if you don't."

He looked up at me and shouted, "Do you really think you're going to wear that?"

I looked down at my black dress pants that were flowing around my sandals that were pretty and summery. I looked at my soft blue crepe shirt and the scarf that matched my accessories and wondered what was happening. Why was he telling me this?

"You look ridiculous. I'm not going anywhere with you!" he shouted.

I looked down, turned around and headed back up the stairs to change. I tried on one outfit after another and struggled to get his approval. Each time, I was faced with the same oppressive spirit. I was told I was fat, unattractive, I embarrassed him, he was going alone.

Biting my lip, I headed back inside and tried not to cry. He followed me into the kitchen and shouted, "I thought I told you to get that kitchen floor cleaned. It looks as stupid as you do."

"You can't do anything right," he continued. "I'm showering and leaving. You've got work here to do. It better look cleaner than this when I get back," he said hovering over me.

I turned to him and answered, "I washed this floor on my hands and knees last night after you barked your order."

"You are so stupid. How did I ever end up with you? You can't even wash a floor right," he ranted.

He showered, got dressed and slammed the door as he left for his reunion. I wondered how long I had tolerated the behavior that lurked behind the doors of my mind, hovered over my thoughts of self-confidence and jabbed at my everyday acceptance of life in general.

The oppression had begun some ten years earlier when a young man, a drug addict, started working with my spouse. I was not privy to that information until much later. All I knew was that I lived in a world where criticism reigned. Hateful words spewed out at me and my children on a daily basis. We were fat, ugly, no one would ever love us. We were good for nothing, we were unkempt, unkind, and unqualified to do anything correctly.

It wasn't just being told these things continually, it was his attitude toward us. It was cruel and demeaning. It held us back, held us down and kept us oppressed. He was cruel.

Not only was I criticized about how I looked, but I was criticized for the simple things. Things like how I cleaned the floor, ate my food, folded our clothes, said certain words and even how I sneezed.

One of the most crucial points at my house was that he wouldn't allow me to do anything without his permission. I could not hang anything on the walls or paint the walls. I could not tell people personal things about our lives. And I wasn't allowed to do anything without his approval. The control, manipulation and oppression were dark and evil. It lingered when he woke up in the morning, while he was at work, after work, and after he went to bed. It slithered out from every pore of his being and came at us with fierce energy.

There are days I look back and wonder how I ever lived through it. People would ask me, and still do today, "Why didn't you break free? Why didn't you leave him?"

Until you have been in those shoes, you will not understand. I tried to face it, I became weak. Not just weak in my attitude, but physically weak.

I'd tell myself, today is the day I will fight back. But if I said something or stepped towards him, I would endanger myself to another slap, kick, punch or push. Oppression constantly won out in my world.

Until one day, after twenty years of abuse, violence and the dark spirit that controlled us, I walked up to the door of freedom that was blocked by oppression. With God's strength and my desperate faith, I busted it down.

It took God, several strong Christ-followers, the police, my parents and my pastor to help me, but I took my children and broke free. I left. It wasn't easy, and several times I was almost pulled back through the door to the wrong side, my past, but God was with me. He pushed me forward. Guilt, lack of confidence, fear and sadness weighed heavily upon me and my girls like a cold wet blanket. But nothing, I repeat, nothing, was as horrible as the oppression.

How does one explain oppression? The dictionary describes it as, *"prolonged cruel or unjust treatment or control."*

God is not for oppression. He does not stand for it. God is a God of freedom. He sent His Son, Jesus, to die on the cross to bust through the doors of control, cruelty, and oppression.

Psalm 9:7-10 states: *"The Lord reigns forever; He has established His throne for judgment. He rules the world in righteousness and judges the peoples with equity. The Lord is a refuge for the oppressed, a stronghold in times of trouble. Those who know Your name trust in You, for You, Lord, have never forsaken those who seek You."*

If you have ever lived under an oppressive spirit from someone like a spouse, parent, child, neighbor or boss, you understand the misery that is connected to being held down and held back. But you were never created to live under cruel tyrannical control. You are meant to live a free, abundant life, filled with blessings and good things from God.

> You are meant to live a free, abundant life, filled with blessings and good things from God.

There is a story that teaches us important truths about busting through doors of oppression that is found in the book of Judges. For twenty years, the Israelites were under the rule of King Jabin, and experienced the most cruel oppression.

But God provided a door of freedom, an opportunity was provided to be led to break free from under the horrid oppression. Unfortunately, like me, it took twenty years for the Israelites to figure out they needed to break free and how to accomplish that feat.

It took great faith and courage to break free from my abuser. But it also took obedience and wisdom. This is what we will learn from this power-packed story, because these are the tools that Judge Deborah used to break oppression.

In this story taken from Judges 4-5, we observe oppression weighing heavily on God's people, the Israelites. We read about a judge named Deborah, who was also a prophetess, a strong leader, a warrior and a wise counsel. She was the leader of Israel during the story, and for the forty years that followed.

God used Deborah in a mighty way to help His people bust down the door of the oppression.

God was pleased that Deborah sought Him in *prayer*, believed Him in *faith*, followed Him in *obedience*, and praised Him in *freedom*.

Let me set up the story for you. God delivered the Israelites from Pharaoh. They went through the wilderness for forty years. Now they were living in the Promised Land, Canaan.

When Joshua *(led the Israelites out of the wilderness to the Promised Land)* died, he left the Israelites with a commission: Conquer Canaan, honor the agreement made with God to obey His laws, then you will receive His protection and blessing.

But the people didn't do it. They liked the Canaanite women. They worshiped the Canaanite gods. They liked how they lived a life free of the rules of Moses.

Oppression does this. It comes in making everything look lovely. You're a nice man, you're my only hope of marriage, I thought. And bam ... the door of oppression was opened and there I lived for the next twenty years.

For the Israelites, they thought, "We're here in the Promised Land. We don't feel like fighting. We're tired. Things don't look so bad. The women look great, the rules look free." But freedom was not to be had for any of them. It was a lie from the pit of Hell.

They abandoned God's laws. They fell into the same pattern they had owned before. Their pattern throughout history looked something like this:

First, they sin *(in this story they worshipped Canaan's idols).*

Next, God punished them by sending oppression through a nation/ leader *(in this story it is King Jabin).*

After the oppression, Israelites repent and asked/begged God for help.

Lastly, God forgave them and sent a hero to help *(in this story, the hero will surprise you).*

Each time the Israelites repented of their sins and asked God for deliverance from the attackers, God sent a leader called a judge *(ruler or leader)* to help them get out of their troubles.

Our story has an unlikely leader. One that frequently gets dismissed, or swept under the rug. Why? Because she is a woman. Not only is she a woman, but Scripture is clear ... she is the Leader of Israel! No human can deny that God planned for His nation to led by a woman. And for forty years, no less.

The good news is that this leader has great steps for us that she laid out clearly so we could learn, grow, and mature in our faith.

Pastor and author John Ortberg says, *"The book of Judges is to reveal and ever so slowly teach Israel and eventually humanity, there is a moral and spiritual reality underneath this world and that finding it and conforming to it is the ultimate battle for you and me and our world."*

The oppression was real. The oppression was strong. The oppressed were begging God for help.

Look Up: Judges 4:1-3
"Again the Israelites did evil in the eyes of the Lord, now that Ehud was dead (Ehud was a previous judge who had freed the people from eighteen years of foreign rule before Deborah was the leader). *So the Lord sold them into the hands of Jabin, King of Canaan, who reigned in Hazor."*

God was trying to get His people to leave their sin. He allowed the oppression in this instance, so they would seek Him. But don't think for a minute that every situation of oppression is God allowing some evil abuser to bring people back to Him.

This world is full of sin and sinners, and there are many abusers who crush the hearts, spirits and lives of others just because they are evil. God allows it and we don't always understand why.

"Sisera, the commander of his army, was based in Harosheth Haggoyim. Because he had nine hundred chariots fitted with iron (this is important) *and had **cruelly oppressed** the Israelites for twenty years, they cried to the Lord for help."*

Here, once again, was the Israelites pattern. Sin/Trouble/Cry for Help/ Salvation. Repeat.

Enter the desperate scene—Judge Deborah. Deborah lived about 1150 BC, approximately a century after the Hebrews had entered Canaan.

Look Up: Judges 4:4-5
"Now Deborah, a prophet, the wife of Lappidoth, (this is all we know

about Deborah's family—there is no mention of children) *was leading Israel at that time.*

"She held court under the Palm of Deborah between Ramah and Bethel (Ramah and Bethel were in the southern part of the land near Judah) *in the hill country of Ephraim, and the Israelites went up to her to have their disputes decided."*

Deborah was a wise counsel and was also known as a prophetess. In Scripture, prophets *(or prophetess in this instance)* heard directly from God. Those whom God gave the gift of prophecy in the Old Testament, such as Elijah, Micah, Jeremiah, and Daniel, had words that were recorded as Scripture. They received their message directly from God as they proclaimed, *"Thus saith the Lord,"* and this was how He gave His directives.

Scripture says this about God's prophets in Amos 3:7, *"Surely the Sovereign Lord does nothing without revealing His plan to His servants the prophets."*

Because Deborah was a prophet, she sought God. This was her daily habit. He would speak to her, she would follow Him.

God directed Deborah to call her general, Barak, and planned for an attack on the evil oppressor, King Jabin. They were going to face the door.

If we are to become wise and use wisdom in everyday life to avoid the trap of control and oppression, we will make a habit of seeking God.

Look Up: Judges 4:6-8
"She sent for Barak son of Abinoam from Kedesh in Naphtali and said to him, 'The Lord, the God of Israel, commands you: Go, take with you ten thousand men of Naphtali and Zebulun and lead them up to Mount

Tabor. I will lead Sisera, the commander of Jabin's army, with his chariots and his troops to the Kishon River and give him into your hands.'

"Barak said to her, 'If you go with me, I will go; but if you don't go with me, I won't go.'"

This was important. Barak was honest with his leader, Judge Deborah. The door of oppression was mighty. It was big, it was powerful, it was going to be tough to bust down. Barak was afraid.

Barak didn't want to lead without her. Kind of a chicken, he was determined not to lead the army alone. The mighty judge, leader, warrior, Deborah heard from God through **prayer**. She had the directive, so her next step was *faith*.

When we believe that God is bigger than our mountains, stronger than our giants, and more powerful than the Enemy, His power is released. He needs you to step forward in **obedience** and show your faith by trusting in His power. Oppression **can be** taken down.

'Certainly I will go with you,' said Deborah."

Certainly means, *"without any doubt."* There was no hesitation there. Deborah, a woman, was not afraid to go out into battle. Why? Because she sought God, and she had faith.

She didn't hesitate, she didn't crumble in fear, she just acted in faith. Because God told her what to do, there was no doubt that she was ready to face the army of 900 chariots with Barak and their 10,000 men. No questions. No complaints. No groanings.

The Israelites didn't have big iron chariots that were powerful and protective. The enemy did. The Israelites didn't have a king and all of his staff and armies. The enemy did.

Throughout history, God didn't let His people come up against the mountains of trials with big fanfare. He didn't provide His people with great power and strength, tools and armies, that would help them win. Instead, it seems it has always been about the underdog. Because God always received the glory when the underdog went in with a staff and some faith (Moses), or a slingshot and little stones (David and Goliath), or a heartfelt plea (Esther).

God took the meek, the humble, the incompetent, and used their willing hearts, their prayers, their pleas, and their faith, to take down all the evil the enemy had to offer.

Deborah was a woman. Most people wouldn't assume that a woman would say, "Sure, I'm in. I'll go out onto the battlefield with you and let's do some battling!" Unless of course you're the Bionic Woman, Wonder Woman, or Super Girl. But remember, Deborah TRUSTED God, and He was telling her ... *do it.*

Barak didn't have that same faith. Deborah let him know what would happen next.

Look Up: Judges 4:9-10
"But because of the course you are taking (cowardly), *the honor will not be yours, for the Lord will deliver Sisera* (commander of King Jabin) *into the hands of a woman."*

Are you thinking that Sisera will be delivered to Deborah? (**Spoiler Alert:** It's a different woman!)

"So Deborah went with Barak to Kedesh. There Barak summoned Zebulun and Naphtali, and ten thousand men went up under his command. Deborah also went up with him."

I like that about Deborah. She was bold. She was courageous. She *sought*

God and she *trusted* God. Now, she and her people were *obeying* God. And, she not only went up to Kedesh with her general, she continued on in the battlefield, and headed straight for the door of oppression!

Within my own circumstances, when I began to seek God in prayer and trust Him with my life and that of my children, I began to hear through promptings of the Holy Spirit. Within my own heart, through Scripture and through others, I heard that I would need to take steps to remove myself from the violence at my home.

As I sought God, I prayed to discover the reasons why my husband, who had always been critical and abusive, had changed so drastically to be so vehemently oppressive.

It all came out in the wash like a pair of muddy jeans. All of the truth came rushing out as I discovered my spouse was operating a crystal meth lab with his drug-addict friend. I found out that he had been unfaithful to me on several occasions, that he was selling drugs using my vehicle, and that he had endangered my children by taking them to his meth lab.

The door called me. The obstacle of oppression taunted me. You're not strong enough. You have no money. You will lose your job as worship director. You won't leave.

I was in the battle. I was on the battlefield. It was not Barak at my side, but my friends and family. It was not me leading the charge, but God was leading and directing. I did not doubt, I trusted and obeyed.

Prayer. Trust. Obedience. I faced the door of oppression.

Hebrews 10:39 states, "*But we do not belong to those who shrink back and are destroyed, but to those who have faith and are saved.*"

Look Up: Judges 4:11-12

"Now Heber the Kenite had left the other Kenites, the descendants of Hobab, Moses' brother-in-law, and pitched his tent by the great tree in Zaanannim near Kedesh."

You might be asking yourself, huh? I don't get it. I thought we were following Deborah and Barak into the battlefield. They were facing the door of oppression. Who's Heber? But this character Heber was important. He was a traitor to the Israelites. He revealed the Israelites' plan to their enemy, the king.

"When they (assumed Heber and his friends) *told Sisera that Barak son of Abinoam had gone up to Mount Tabor, Sisera summoned from Harosheth Haggoyim to the Kishon River all his men and his nine hundred chariots fitted with iron."*

Face the door and expect the Enemy to bring out the big guns. He does not want you headed to *freedom.*

Israel didn't have iron chariots. Instead, they had horses and swords. Already the bad guys had the big advantage.

Look Up: Judges 4:14-18

"Then Deborah said to Barak, 'Go! This is the day the Lord has given Sisera into your hands. Has not the Lord gone ahead of you?' So Barak went down Mount Tabor, with ten thousand men following him. At Barak's advance, the Lord routed Sisera and all his chariots and army by the sword, and Sisera got down from his chariot and fled on foot."

Remember, Sisera had cruelly oppressed the Israelites for twenty years. That was a long time to be cruel and unkind. Now, he was running for his life.

"Barak pursued the chariots and army as far as Harosheth Haggoyim,

and all Sisera's troops fell by the sword; not a man was left. Sisera, meanwhile, fled on foot to the tent of Jael, the wife of Heber the Kenite, because there was an alliance between Jabin king of Hazor and the family of Heber the Kenite."

There was Heber the Kenite again. He wasn't trusted. He was a traitor. He was with the King and his awful commander, Sisera. The Kenites were not part of the Israelite tribe or beliefs. They were tent dwellers, nomads. They roamed the hills. We would think of them today as vagabonds.

"Jael (Heber's wife) *went out to meet Sisera and said to him, 'Come, my lord, come right in. Don't be afraid.' So he entered her tent, and she covered him with a blanket."*

During that time, a woman wasn't allowed to have any man in her tent except her husband. But Sisera was desperate for help and a place to hide. And he was the leader so expected help from the Kenites.

Unfortunately for Sisera, Jael's family lineage was aligned with Israel. She remained loyal to them and undid her husband's betrayal.

Look Up: Judges 4:19-23
"'I'm thirsty,' he (Sisera) *said. 'Please give me some water.' She opened a skin of milk, gave him a drink, and covered him up.*

'Stand in the doorway of the tent,' he told her. 'If someone comes by and asks you, Is anyone in there? say 'No.'

"But Jael, Heber's wife, picked up a tent peg and a hammer and went quietly to him while he lay fast asleep, exhausted. She drove the peg through his temple into the ground, and he died.

"Just then Barak came by in pursuit of Sisera, and Jael went out to meet

him. 'Come,' she said, 'I will show you the man you're looking for.' So he went in with her, and there lay Sisera with the tent peg through his temple—dead.

"On that day God subdued Jabin king of Canaan before the Israelites. And the hand of the Israelites pressed harder and harder against Jabin king of Canaan until they destroyed him."

The door was faced. Opportunity for freedom called loudly through the voice of God. The woman-leader answered boldly, "Yes, I'm here, God. We'll trust and obey."

The battle was won. The wise leader, Deborah, had listened to God, trusted God, and obeyed God. She told Barak that the victory would not go to him but would end up in the hands of a woman. That woman, Jael, killed the evil villain, Sisera, and Israel destroyed the horrible King Jabin.

Door busted. Oppression pushed aside. You see when Jesus Christ died for you and me on the cross, oppression was crushed when they pounded the nails through His hands and feet and His blood flowed freely. Oppression was destroyed when He took His last breath and died, and when they pierced His side. Oppression was demolished when the stone was rolled away from the tomb and Christ arose. Freedom arrived in full force.

Oppression has no right over you. It says it does. You think it does. People will tell you that it does. "You can't leave! You can help him." That's what my church elder board told me.

But the police said, "You will be charged as an accomplice, and in most instances like yours, we'll find you or your children dead if you don't leave."

Martin Luther King Jr. once said, *"The ultimate tragedy is not the oppression and cruelty by the bad people but the silence over that by the good people."*

Many were silent when I told them what had happened to me. Many refused to believe me. Many walked away. But God never left me, and I broke through to freedom. I have never forgotten who was there beside me.

You might think the story is over. Deborah *prayed*. Deborah *trusted*. Deborah *obeyed* and had the freedom to lead the way to the door. But wait ... there's more!

In Judges Chapter 5, we find *The Song of Deborah*. This poem, written no doubt by Deborah herself, continued to teach how to bust down the door of oppression.

Look Up: Judges 5:1-3
"On that day Deborah and Barak son of Abinoam sang this song: 'When the princes in Israel take the lead, when the people willingly offer themselves—praise the Lord! Hear this, you kings! Listen, you rulers! I, even I, will sing to the Lord; I will praise the Lord, the God of Israel, in song.'"

In Judges Chapter 5 we learn a few more details about what happened in this story. We discover that God sent a rainstorm during the battle and that the *wadi, (a valley or channel that is dry except in the rainy season)* of the Kishon River, was flooded. As I studied about the Kishon River, I learned that it was frequently dry and even known as a little brook. Its waters head into the Mediterranean Sea. Sisera was so proud of his chariots that he never suspected they would become stuck in the mud.

Therefore, the unlikely army of Israelites, battling with only horses and swords, were the winners. The chariots became a liability instead of an asset with the floods, and evil lost. Oppression was defeated.

Look Up: Judges 5:20-21, 31
"From the heavens the stars fought, from their courses they fought against Sisera. The river Kishon swept them away, the age-old river, the river Kishon. March on, my soul; be strong!"

In those verses we see Judge Deborah's final step to busting down the door of oppression. Glory was given to God. Praise, honor, and glory to the One who gave them the power to banish the evil. She didn't take the praise for herself. She certainly didn't give it to Barak or Jael. Instead, she gave all glory to God.

The battle was the Lord's and He blessed them by having them win. Today, God continues to use the unlikely to do powerful work for Him.

"'So may all your enemies perish, Lord! But may all who love you be like the sun when it rises in its strength.' Then the land had peace forty years."

While Deborah, who helped bust down the door of oppression, was in office there was peace in Israel for exactly forty years. No oppression.

While we may believe the lies of the Enemy and continue to survive under the dictatorship of oppression, we can battle and break free. The steps are laid out for us within this story.

Great leaders throughout scripture took the same steps to conquer trouble, led others, and lived a Godly life. Women like Deborah, men like Moses, children like Samuel, all relied on the wisdom of God, received it from Him, trusted Him, obeyed Him and praised Him.

FOUR STEPS TO BUST THROUGH THE DIFFICULT DOOR OF OPPRESSION:

STEP ONE: *Seek God,* have a submissive attitude.

Going to God in prayer over big concerns and small concerns alike, is an essential part of being a Christ-follower. Maturity in our relationship with God relies on us reading His Word, having conversations in prayer with Him, and seeking Him for direction. We must do this to lead our best life.

> **I Chronicles 16:11,** *"Look to the Lord and His strength; seek His face always."*

> **II Chronicles 7:14,** *"If My people, who are called by My name, will humble themselves and pray and seek My face and turn from their wicked ways, then I will hear from heaven, and I will forgive their sin and will heal their land."*

> **Acts 17:27,** *"God did this so that they would seek Him and perhaps reach out for Him and find Him, though He is not far from any one of us."*

STEP TWO: *Trust God,* have a faithful heart.

The whole premise of Christianity is that we have faith and believe that God the Father is the Creator of our being. He sent His Son to die for us. He loves us more than we can comprehend. His plans are for good and for an abundant life. When we fully trust Him with every single aspect of our life, then true freedom begins.

> **Psalm 9:10,** *"Those who know Your name trust in You, for You, Lord, have never forsaken those who seek You."*

> **Psalm 31:14,** *"But I trust in You, Lord; I say, 'You are my God.'"*

Romans 8:28, *"And we know that in all things God works for the good of those who love Him, who have been called according to His purpose."*

STEP THREE: *Obey God,* have a servant spirit.

Obedience is important to God. Throughout Scripture, when He gave a command to His people, He expected them to obey. Not because He is an oppressive tyrant, but because He had their good in mind ... always. We need to learn to obey God because what He has in store for us is far better than what we could plan for ourselves.

Deuteronomy 11:1, *"Love the Lord your God and keep His requirements, His decrees, His laws and His commands always."*

John 15:14, *"You are my friends if you do what I command."*

Revelation 14:12, *"This calls for patient endurance on the part of the people of God who keep His commands and remain faithful to Jesus."*

STEP FOUR: *Praise God,* have a humble attitude.

When good things happen and we play a part in that good thing, it's easy to want to take the credit. Look at me, I did something great! But God is clear that He wants the glory. When we have humility at the forefront of our attitudes, we will happily give God the praise, honor, and glory that is due Him in every good situation.

Exodus 15:2, *"The Lord is my strength and my defense; He has become my salvation. He is my God, and I will praise Him, my father's God, and I will exalt Him."*

Psalm 75:1, *"We praise you, God, we praise You, for Your name is near; people tell of Your wonderful deeds."*

> **Isaiah 63:7,** *"I will tell of the kindnesses of the Lord, the deeds for which He is to be praised, according to all the Lord has done for us—yes, the many good things He has done for Israel, according to His compassion and many kindnesses."*

We need to learn to seek God for everything, but we need to be especially faithful in remembering that nothing is too big for God. When we rely on His power, we can accomplish anything He sets out for us to accomplish!

If you have experienced oppression within your own life, and have attained freedom, you know what I know—there is no greater joy than to live in freedom!

But perhaps you are still under the horribly evil reign of oppression. It's time to begin a plan that will allow you to get to the battlefield and face the door. But you must start by seeking God in prayer.

I came across an inspiring bit of history. One of the greatest leaders we have had in America, our first president, George Washington, displayed incredible leadership. But his gift of leading, battling evil, and abolishing oppression had always begun with the key step we learned from Judge Deborah ... meet with God in prayer.

In an 1824 book entitled, *The Life of Washington*, Anna C. Reed from the American Sunday School Union, wrote this about Washington at Valley Forge:

> *"The inhabitants of the surrounding country, knowing this sad state of the army, were very uneasy; one of them left his home, one day, and as he was passing thoughtfully the edge of a wood near the hut-camp, he heard low sounds of a voice. He stopped to listen, and looking between the trunks of the large trees he*

saw Gen. Washington engaged in prayer. He passed quietly on, that he might not disturb him; and, on returning home, told this family he knew the Americans would succeed, for their leader did not trust in his own strength, but sought aid from the hearer of prayer, who promised in His word, 'Call upon me in the day of trouble; I will deliver thee, and thou shalt glorify me.'"

God always gives us His Word to encourage our hearts. If you are dealing with oppression today, write this verse down, memorize it, and tack it up in your home, in your car, and anywhere you can remind yourself of its comforting message.

Jeremiah 20:13, *"Sing to the Lord! Praise the Lord! He rescues the oppressed from the power of evil people"* (GNT).

To lead others or ourselves out of danger and oppression is no small feat. But with God, we have the power we need to accomplish anything. It's time to begin with four simple steps that will help us combat an evil door—oppression: *pray, trust, obey and praise.*

The battle belongs to the Lord! Get ready, you're headed to battle where with God at your side, there's a big door that will be busted open!

Questions:

1. Why do you think God chose a woman to lead Israel for forty years? What characteristics about Deborah did you see in this passage that made you encouraged and inspired by her attitudes and behavior?

2. Have you ever experienced a situation where you felt oppressed? Describe three emotions you felt while walking through that experience.

3. Have you, or anyone you know, ever felt paralyzed when dealing with an evil situation where you/they didn't know how to break free? What did you/they do?

4. Is there a situation today that you have been in where you need to break free? If so, what steps will you take to begin the process of getting ready to bust down the door of oppression to freedom? How will you combat your fears?

Look Up:

1. Psalm 13:5

2. Psalm 84:12

3. I Chronicles 16:28

4. John 14:15

5. Romans 1:5

6. Ephesians 1:5

7. Philippians 1:6

Songs:

Hymn ~ *"Trust and Obey"* (John Sammis and Daniel Towner)

Contemporary ~ *"Joy of the Lord"* (Ed Cash and Rend Collective)

Closing Prayer:

Dear Jesus,

God, help us to be wise in our endeavors.
Help us to trust You in the challenges.

Give us strength to be courageous
like Deborah and obey You.

And above all, help us to remain humble
and to praise You for every good thing.

In Jesus' Name, *Amen.*

Jesus Christ: Door Buster

*"There is no other One who did more to overcome
all obstacles to get mankind to freedom.
When Jesus Christ died on the cross, the final obstacle hindering
the door to freedom was busted down for us all."*

Kathy A. Weckwerth

Door Busted: In our last lesson, we learned from Deborah that oppression can be ugly, evil and very powerful. It can keep us believing that we are worthless and unable to break free from its powerful hold. But God helps us face the door, bust through and overcome it. We can obtain freedom and live an abundant life, just as God desires for us.

John 3:16, *"For God so loved the world, that he gave His only Son, that whoever believes in Him should not perish but have eternal life."*

The waitress set steaming hot cups of coffee in front of me and my two giggling girlfriends. "Anything else, girls?" she asked. We shook our heads no and continued with our time of catching up.

I dreaded what I knew was to come ... the ultimate question, "How are you really doing?" would be next. My friend, Kathleen, gently and gingerly launched into the question. "So, my honey, how are you really doing?"

I took the next fifteen minutes to cover the details of my ministry, the church, the latest speaking event and my family. My friend, Tammy said, "Okay. That's great. Now, what's happening with you?"

As I spent time being authentic and painfully honest, I admitted that after these twenty-plus years, there are moments where I continue to face my own doors of rejection, challenges, fear, doubt, and unforgiveness.

I looked at them and said, "I still get angry about what happened to me. I still get angry that my ex-spouse could run a drug lab and not pay for the crime. But I am most angry that he tried to take my middle child's life, and the judge let him off with a slap on the wrist."

I had recently listened to my oldest daughter tell me of her father's continual failure to be a dad to her and her sisters. Disappointment, frustration, and quite honestly, unchartered waters of rage were tossing about inside of me.

Each one of us at that table could hear it, and each one of us knew I needed help.

"I think you should go talk to someone, Kathy," Tammy advised.

"Yes, I agree," Kathleen concurred, "You can't keep coming up against this each time he does something else to let you guys down. You need to face it and deal with it."

"I don't know anyone who could help, and I don't trust anyone," I answered.

Then I suddenly remembered a friend of mine connected to a church I had served many years ago. I sipped my coffee and reassured them, "I'll think about calling someone."

Deep inside I didn't want to do it. I walked past that same door over and over. I looked at it, I stared at it, I wondered about it, and then I'd walk away. After all, I wasn't the one who had broken up the family, hurt all of us, and continued to try to control us.

That night, driving home on that dark, cool fall evening, I told myself it was time. Time to walk up to the door, time to realize what really stood between me and freedom. Time to see the obstacle and bust down a door. I knew what it was. I just didn't want to admit it. I had an unforgiving spirit.

The next morning, I dialed the number of my friend who had a counseling ministry and said, "Richard, we need to talk. I need help."

Richard led a wonderful ministry where Godly leaders prayed with hurting people, counseled them, and helped set them free from their troubles. I had referred many people to him, but I hadn't made an appointment for myself to see him for over fifteen years.

Several weeks after coffee with the girlfriends, I drove into Richard's driveway and prepared to meet him and another counselor for a three-hour session. Richard, the kind and gentle leader, opened the door to his home, and we prayed and began our time together.

He read Scripture, made time for prayers, and listened intently to my rantings, ravings, and ramblings. At times, the other counselor added in a thought or offered a prayer. I felt things were going splendidly.

That is until Richard asserted, "I don't think we're getting to the root of the problem, Kathy. God is telling me I need to do something else."

What? I wondered at what we were missing. I watched as Richard went to the kitchen and pulled out a chair from under the dinette table. He placed the chair very close to me, sat in it and faced me. I will never forget the words he said, or the moments that followed as we walked through the pain together.

Richard took my hands in his and said, "Kathy, I am going to be your ex-spouse."

I looked at him incredulously and thought ... what! "No!" I exclaimed. "Richard, you can be anyone in my life. Anyone. But you can't be him."

He continued, "I am him now. Listen to my words."

Richard began to ask for forgiveness for all of the horrible things my ex-spouse had done. He painstakingly listed them one by one. The unfaithfulness. The physical, mental and emotional abuse. The attempt on my daughter's life. All were included as a part of the sincere apology he offered up in the place of my ex.

I sat straight-faced and felt a chilly snowy-ice around my mind and spirit that began to rise up around me like snow accumulation on a winter's day.

I listened. He apologized. And when it was all over, he asked, "Can you forgive me?"

Silence.

"Can you say something? Say something, Kathy," Richard stated emphatically.

The pain, the hurt, the bitterness rose up within me and began to burst at the door of my being. I felt a single cold wet tear slide down my cheek. I felt the bitterness slither and slide underneath my threshold. Boom ... the door was thrust open and out it came. The ugliness. The resentment. The cold heart. The bitterness. The contempt. The unforgiveness. I cried out, "I hate you. I hate you. I hate you!"

And there it was. Shocked, I looked at my friend, who was not shocked at all and I exclaimed emphatically, "Oh, Richard! I'm so sorry. Where did that come from?!"

Richard calmly spoke the words I will never forget, "Now, we are getting somewhere. Now, God can do His work." And He did.

I asked Jesus to forgive me. I prayed, I cried, I forgave. The grace, mercy, and forgiveness extended to me by Christ's death on the cross, gave me the power to face the door and its ugly obstacles. I asked God to give me the strength, courage and power to bust down the door. Freedom had been calling me. But notice, God did not do it for me. He did it with me.

God will never, ever force you to do anything. He operates with a major rule that He has followed since He created Adam and Eve. It's the rule of ... *free will.*

> You must willingly make the choice to step towards that opportunity and face the obstacles.
>
>

When you determine that you are ready to look at your doors of opportunity, you see what God is calling you to do. You must willingly make the choice to step towards that opportunity and face the obstacles.

God has given you charge over your own life. You don't get to decide what others will do, only what you will do. Once you are headed to that door, it is essential that you face it. By admitting that you need God's help, you have already begun door buster preparation.

Holocaust survivor, Corrie Ten Boom once said, *"I know that the experiences of our lives, when we let God use them, become the mysterious and perfect preparation for the work He will give us to do."*

God never wastes our experiences. Each thing you walk through, each thing you survive, is another experience that you can use to help others who may go through similar situations.

The Apostle Paul says in II Corinthians 1:3-4, *"Praise be to the God and Father of our Lord Jesus Christ, the Father of compassion and the God of all comfort, who comforts us in all our troubles, so that we can comfort those in any trouble with the comfort we ourselves receive from God."*

Throughout this book, we've looked at many obstacles that can stand in front of the doors of our lives. We've studied insurmountable challenges, social pressures, rejection and discouragement. These are all difficult obstacles. But for me personally, the most difficult to bust through was the door of unforgiveness.

Blinded by the Enemy, we remain at a distance from our doors. We long for freedom. We desire new experiences. But, between us and the door lies the obstacle that makes it so incredibly difficult. We have to work to break through. Frequently in life, we're not drawn to things that make us work. But what great God-things are we missing because we aren't making an effort?

God is calling to us from behind the doors. He sent His Son, Jesus, to earth to be an example of how to live life to the fullest, how to respond to difficulties and trials, and how to answer the doors. After all, Jesus Christ experienced every single one of the obstacles we discussed in each lesson of this book. Yet, He did it with grace, with mercy, and with faith. How can you and I become more like Christ?

When we look at the last door Jesus faced ... death on the cross, we can understand at a deeper level what it means to bust down doors.

Jesus describes Himself as the Good Shepherd. He knows His sheep and His sheep know His voice when He calls to them. Living on a farm, I learned about sheep. Of all the domestic animals, sheep are the most helpless. Sheep can spend their entire day grazing on grass, never looking up to see where they are or where they're going. They often become lost. They won't defend themselves, they won't run away, instead they huddle together and are an easy target for their enemies.

Sheep are totally dependent on their shepherd. They know his voice. When creating a sheep pen at night, a shepherd would put together a rough circle of rocks piled into the shape of a wall with a small open space to enter. At nightfall, the shepherd would drive the sheep through the gate. Since there was no gate to close, the shepherd would keep the sheep in and the wild animals out by lying across the opening. He would sleep there, literally becoming the door to the sheep.

When scripture refers to us as sheep and Jesus as the Good Shepherd, we understand that He wants us to become a part of His fold. A part of His flock. He calls to us.

When Jesus offers Himself up as a living sacrifice for mankind, He becomes one of the sheep. He becomes the Lamb of God who takes away the sins of the world. Jesus offers us, behind the door of sin, the gift of salvation. In order to understand the fact that God called Him to the Ultimate Door, the door of death for our salvation, we need to look at His journey in the last days of His life.

Jesus began the journey. He is God, but because He was also man, He experienced the same emotions that we do. In Matthew Chapter 26, we read that Jesus was on His knees praying in the Garden of Gethsemane. In those moments, He faced the door of the unknown.

Look Up: Matthew 26:36-38
"Then Jesus went with His disciples to a place called Gethsemane, and He said to them, 'Sit here while I go over there and pray.' He took Peter and the two sons of Zebedee along with Him, and He began to be sorrowful and troubled. Then He said to them, 'My soul is overwhelmed with sorrow to the point of death. Stay here and keep watch with Me.'"

Jesus had just finished having His last Passover meal with the disciples. Judas Iscariot, the one who betrayed the Savior, left the meal to sell Jesus' whereabouts for thirty pieces of silver. Eight of His disciples remained at that spot, while He took Peter, James and John with Him.

Gethsemane was east of Jerusalem on the Mount of Olives and this was the third time that Jesus singled out Peter, James and John to accompany Him. Perhaps with a deep hope that they could accompany Him to the most difficult door of all ... *death.*

Since Jesus was also God *(they are part of the Trinity of Father, Son and Holy Spirit)*, Jesus knew what would happen. The human part of Him didn't know what the pain of being crucified would be like. Jesus was completely overwhelmed, so much so, that He was sweating drops of blood.

Look Up: Luke 22:44
"And being in anguish, He prayed more earnestly, and His sweat was like drops of blood falling to the ground."

You might wonder how it is humanly possible to sweat drops of blood, after all, He had a human body. *Hematidrosis* is a known physical condition where capillary blood vessels that feed the sweat glands rupture, causing them to exude blood. This occurs under extreme conditions of physical or emotional stress.

Not only was Jesus facing the obstacles in front of the door, but He was experiencing all of the emotions that we face when God calls us to a door.

Look Up: Matthew 26:39
"Going a little farther, He fell with His face to the ground and prayed, 'My

Father, if it is possible, may this cup be taken from Me. Yet not as I will, but as You will.'"

He moved closer to the door. The door will bring freedom from sin for mankind. The door was blocked with all the obstacles that we've studied in these past nine lessons: The Unknown, Rejection, Attitude, Insurmountable Challenges, Fear of Social Pressures, Values and Beliefs, Waves of Doubt, Discouragement and Oppression.

Did you think when you started reading this book that you had to be brave all by yourself? Did you believe that you would be able to bust down doors without help? Or have you been so afraid of any new opportunities, that you avoid any doors altogether?

In Scripture, Jesus wanted to avoid the door. He was asking in the previous passage for God to take this opportunity from Him. He doesn't want it. Not really. Who would? A sinless Son dies for sinful man. It doesn't seem like a door anyone would want to bust down.

But Jesus was willing. Ultimately, obedience led Him to the door that needed to be broken down, pushed open, walked through, and God allowed freedom and forgiveness to flow freely.

Look Up: Matthew 26:40-42
"Then He returned to His disciples and found them sleeping. 'Couldn't you men keep watch with Me for one hour?' he asked Peter. 'Watch and pray so that you will not fall into temptation. The spirit is willing, but the flesh is weak.'

"He went away a second time and prayed, 'My Father, if it is not possible for this cup to be taken away unless I drink it, may your will be done.'"

If you have been suffering from guilt and wondering why you didn't want to face a door or deal with an obstacle and trying (or try) to bust it down to get to God ... *stop it.* Stop with the guilty conscience. That doesn't come from God. It's okay to question Him. It's okay to be afraid. We just read that His own Son, Jesus questioned Him and was scared. The most important thing to remember is that Jesus experienced those emotions, and yet still remained faithful to the call.

Here's what I have learned about the doors. One can understand it very clearly when you read these verses. Other people are NOT called to our doors ... we are. If we expect them to accompany us, do the work with us and for us, we're mistaken.

God lays out a plan for each one of us, so that each one of us will have the opportunity to answer Him and fulfill the call. Jesus wanted His friends to be with Him, help Him walk through it, and help bust down the door But, in the end, only Jesus could do the work. And in the end, only you can do the work God calls you to accomplish.

As Jesus was in the Garden, his friends were fast asleep. Judas delivered Jesus into the hands of the Roman soldiers.

Look Up: Matthew 26:48-50
"Now the betrayer had arranged a signal with them: 'The one I kiss is the man; arrest him.' Going at once to Jesus, Judas said, 'Greetings, Rabbi!' and kissed Him.

"Jesus replied, 'Do what you came for, friend.'"

Talk about rejection! Scripture tells us that once the soldiers arrested Him, all of Jesus' disciples ran away.

Look Up: Matthew 26:56b
"Then all the disciples deserted Him and fled."

Alone, He faced the obstacles. Instead of a couple things that would block Him, there were many. But He was never really alone, for God never leaves us. *"Be strong and courageous. Do not be afraid or terrified because of them, for the Lord your God goes with you; He will never leave you nor forsake you"* (Deuteronomy 31:6).

When Jesus faced Caiaphas, it was a major obstacle in the way of freedom. He knew that God was prodding Him on through the process, but it was not easy.

Look Up: Matthew 26:63-68
"The high priest said to Him, 'I charge you under oath by the living God: Tell us if you are the Messiah, the Son of God.'

'You have said so,' Jesus replied. 'But I say to all of you: From now on you will see the Son of Man sitting at the right hand of the Mighty One and coming on the clouds of heaven.'

"Then the high priest tore his clothes and said, 'He has spoken blasphemy! Why do we need any more witnesses? Look, now you have heard the blasphemy. What do you think?'

'He is worthy of death,' they answered.

"Then they spit in his face and struck him with their fists. Others slapped him and said, 'Prophesy to us, Messiah. Who hit you?'"

In answer to the Jewish high priest's request as to who Jesus claimed He was, Jesus stated that He would sit at the right hand of God. This was a clear case of blasphemy according to their laws.

One by one, the obstacles we have studied were there. The obstacles that continually block the doors God calls us to were faced by the Savior. The Unknown. Rejection. Attitude. Insurmountable Challenges. Fear of Social Pressures. Values and Beliefs. Waves of Doubt. Discouragement.

Oppression. They were all right there in front of Him. One by one, He looked at them, and got ready to bust them down with His faith and obedience to His Father.

Look Up: Isaiah 53:3-5

"He (Jesus) was despised and rejected by mankind, a man of suffering, and familiar with pain. Like one from whom people hide their faces He was despised, and we held Him in low esteem. Surely He took up our pain and bore our suffering, yet we considered Him punished by God, stricken by Him, and afflicted. But He was pierced for our transgressions, He was crushed for our iniquities; the punishment that brought us peace was on Him, and by His wounds we are healed."

As morning came, Jesus stood before Pontius Pilate, governor of Judea, Samaria, and Idumea from 26-36 A.D. Because the Jews did not have the authority to execute Jesus, they took Him to Pilate.

Look Up: Matthew 27:22-28

"'What shall I do, then, with Jesus who is called the Messiah?' Pilate asked.

"They all answered, 'Crucify Him!'

"'Why? What crime has He committed?' asked Pilate.

"But they shouted all the louder, 'Crucify Him!'

"When Pilate saw that he was getting nowhere, but that instead an uproar was starting, he took water and washed his hands in front of the crowd. 'I am innocent of this man's blood,' he said. 'It is your responsibility!'

"All the people answered, 'His blood is on us and on our children!'

"Then he released Barabbas (a notorious rebel and murderer) *to them. But he had Jesus flogged, and handed Him over to be crucified."*

Pilate hoped that by flogging *(hit or whipped repeatedly)* Jesus would satisfy the anger of the mob. But to fulfill the call, Jesus had to die on the cross.

Look Up: Matthew 27:27-31

"Then the governor's soldiers took Jesus into the Praetorium (the official residence of the governor while in Jerusalem, originally built for Herod the Great) and gathered the whole company of soldiers around Him. They stripped Him and put a scarlet robe on Him, and then twisted together a crown of thorns and set it on His head. They put a staff in His right hand. Then they knelt in front of Him and mocked Him. 'Hail, king of the Jews!' they said. They spit on Him, and took the staff and struck Him on the head again and again. After they had mocked Him, they took off the robe and put His own clothes on Him. Then they led Him away to crucify Him."

He began the journey of carrying the cross. The path was known as the Via Dolorosa or the "Way of Grief." On the way, the soldiers forced a man named Simon from Cyrene to carry the cross for Jesus. The path would lead Him once again to stand right before the final obstacles of the door. Pain. Suffering. Doubt. Oppression. Physical harm.

Look Up: Matthew 27:50

"And when Jesus had cried out again in a loud voice, He gave up His spirit."

Jesus faced the door. Faced the obstacles and then fulfilled His destiny. Isaiah 53:7 says, *"He was oppressed and afflicted, yet He did not open His mouth; He was led like a lamb to the slaughter, and as a sheep before its shearers is silent, so he did not open His mouth."*

The Messiah became like a lamb, offered up as a sacrifice for our sins. The sacrifice would be made once and for all, so that we could experience everlasting life. But the obstacles weren't quite over, for the greatest day in history was not only the day Jesus died on the cross for our sins, but is partnered with the other greatest day in history— the day He rose again.

Look Up: Matthew 28:5-7

"The angel said to the women, 'Do not be afraid, for I know that you are looking for Jesus, who was crucified. He is not here; He has risen, just as He said. Come and see the place where He lay. Then go quickly and tell His disciples: "He has risen from the dead and is going ahead of you into Galilee. There you will see him." Now I have told you.'"

Jesus was the ultimate door buster. The final obstacle was defeated ... death. With the obstacles of sin and death taken down, we have eternal life. Scripture says, *"Where, O death, is your victory? Where, O death, is your sting?"* (I Corinthians 15:55).

Jesus conquered death on the cross and all its obstacles. And then finished it all off by busting down the door completely when He rose from the dead and is seated at the right hand of the Father. *"Since, then, you have been raised with Christ, set your hearts on things above, where Christ is, seated at the right hand of God"* (Colossians 3:1).

Throughout your life, God will provide opportunities for you behind His doors. The prospect of amazing and exciting events is waiting for you. But because we live on Planet Earth and it's filled with sin and sinful people, there will be obstacles that block those doors. Will we be brave enough to ask God to help us get to Him and His plans for us?

Many individuals who were called to face doors, faced huge obstacles. One of my favorite examples was an incredible black botanist, inventor, encourager, and Christ-follower named George Washington Carver. His days were filled with huge obstacles. Nevertheless, God continued to call to him.

Born into slavery in 1855, George faced the challenges of poor health, his mother's death, and not being allowed to attend a nearby school. He often spent his days studying flowers, trees, birds, and bugs. With a strong call from God and motivation to make something of himself, George left home in search of knowledge and became a brilliant botanist who focused his studies on sweet potatoes and peanuts.

George once said, "*I love to think of nature as an unlimited broadcasting station, through which God speaks to us every hour, if we will only tune in.*"

In regard to his studies and inventions, George said this, "*God is going to reveal to us things He never revealed before if we put our hands in His. No books ever go into my laboratory. The thing I am to do and the way of doing it are revealed to me ... The method is revealed to me the moment I am inspired to create something new. Without God to draw aside the curtain I would be helpless.*"

Through no fault of his own, George Washington Carver faced daunting obstacles, busted down their doors, and achieved a plan that God had before George was even born. "*Before I formed you in the womb I knew you, before you were born I set you apart ...*" (Jeremiah 1:5).

There is hope. There are many examples of those who have been called, faced their obstacles and, with God's help, busted down the door to a great future.

God has a plan for your life. He will continue to lay the steps out before you. He never reveals too much at once, because our human selves would be overwhelmed. But little by little He reveals, He unfolds, He prepares, He calls.

FOUR STEPS TO BECOMING A STRONG DOOR BUSTER:

STEP ONE: *Listen* for the call from God.

If God is behind your doors, there will be opportunities for things that are bigger than you can accomplish on your own. It will be greater than your expectations. It will be something fresh and new, outside your comfort zone, and fulfill His plan for your life. Don't run *from* it … run *to* it!

> **Psalm 40:3,** *"He put a new song in my mouth, a hymn of praise to our God. Many will see and fear the Lord and put their trust in Him."*

> **Proverbs 23:18,** *"There is surely a future hope for you, and your hope will not be cut off."*

> **Isaiah 43:19,** *"See, I am doing a new thing! Now it springs up; do you not perceive it? I am making a way in the wilderness and streams in the wasteland."*

STEP TWO: *Look* at the obstacles in front of the door.

Because God is always about growing and stretching your faith, and making you mature in Him, He will allow obstacles to block your doors. Don't turn and run from them. This is a chance to see God at work in your life. Embrace the opportunity by moving forward in faith!

> **Isaiah 26:3,** *"You will keep in perfect peace those whose minds are steadfast, because they trust in You."*

> **Isaiah 41:10,** *"So do not fear, for I am with you; do not be dismayed, for I am your God. I will strengthen you and help you; I will uphold you with my righteous right hand."*

> **John 14:27,** *"Peace I leave with you; My peace I give you. I do not give*

to you as the world gives. Do not let your hearts be troubled and do not be afraid."

STEP THREE: *Lift* your prayers to God for help.

God loves people who display heart attitudes of humility. When you say to God, "You are God and I am not," you give Him the place in your life that He deserves. You relinquish all pride, all control, and admit you need His help. The doors break down faster when you go in with humility.

> **Proverbs 11:2,** *"When pride comes, then comes disgrace, but with humility comes wisdom."*

> **James 4:6,** *"But He gives us more grace. That is why Scripture says: 'God opposes the proud but shows favor to the humble.'"*

> **I Peter 5:6,** *"Humble yourselves, therefore, under God's mighty hand, that He may lift you up in due time."*

STEP FOUR: *Lean* into God with great expectations.

God called to you with an opportunity. You saw the obstacles. You humbled yourself to face the obstacles, and together, you and God have broken through them. The door is now busted down. As you make your way onto the path of the journey God has laid out before you, expect wonderful things. Expect God to show up in ways He's never shown you before. Expect that you will go further, do more, and be blessed in Him. Expect great things!

> **Job 22:28,** *"What you decide on will be done, and light will shine on your ways."*

> **Jeremiah 33:3,** *"Call to me and I will answer you and tell you great and unsearchable things you do not know."*

Ephesians 3:20-21, *"Now to Him who is able to do immeasurably more than all we ask or imagine, according to His power that is at work within us, to Him be glory in the church and in Christ Jesus throughout all generations, forever and ever! Amen."*

The journey of life is so different for each one of us. The path that God takes us on can twist and turn and be filled with bumps and difficult doors. But it can also be one that is filled with excitement, energy, and passion.

There may be moments when you feel afraid of the future or discouraged by the past. There may be days when you think this path, this door, isn't for me. The good news is that God is with you, and He's always ready to help you bust through the doors. He has a plan for your life.

If you're facing a door today with obstacles that block your future, it's time to go before God. It's time to ask Him for help to face the problems, deal with the issues and remove the obstacle. He is on your side and wants you to win the battles.

With each door you bust down, you will become smarter, more faith-filled and more mature in your walk with Christ. You'll experience opportunities, people, and places you never thought you could or would because God has your best life in mind.

Listen today for God's call. *Look* at the door and discover any obstacles. *Lift* your prayers to the One who believes in you. *Lean* into God to bust down the door. He'll help. Become a door buster!

Questions:

1. Why do you think the disciples fell asleep in the Garden of Gethsemane when Jesus needed them so desperately?

2. Do you feel that God has been calling you to do something but there are obstacles that are stopping you? Describe the call. Name the obstacle(s).

3. Name a time when God called you to do something, whether big or little, and you were brave enough to face it and you accomplished the feat. Were you afraid? If so, describe your fear and how you overcame it.

4. After reading this book, list specific steps that you will take to face your obstacles and become a door buster.

Look Up:

1. Psalm 34:17-18

2. Isaiah 30:21

3. Matthew 7:7

4. John 15:5

5. Acts 4:12

6. Philippians 4:19

7. Revelation 3:7-8

Songs:

Hymn ~ *"All the Way My Savior Leads Me"* (Fanny Crosby and Robert Lowry)

Contemporary ~ *"Mighty to Save"* (Reuben Morgan)

Closing Prayer:

Dear Jesus,

Thank you for forgiving my sins.

Thank you for shedding your blood
on the cross so that I can have eternal life.

Help me to always remember
that no matter what obstacle
I come up against in life,

You are always with me to help
bust down that door to get to Your will,
Your plan, and Your freedom on the other side.

In Jesus' name, *Amen.*

Door Busters

About the Author

Kathy Weckwerth is Founder and Executive Director of the nonprofit ministry, Best Life Ministries. She is a pastor, motivational speaker, author, Bible study facilitator, newspaper columnist, and radio host of YOUR BEST with Kathy Weckwerth found on iTunes and Soundcloud. Kathy and her husband, Dean, live in rural Minnesota next door to their 1900's church that serves as Best Life Ministries' headquarters.

Other books by Kathy: *Putting the Pieces Together: A Worship Director's Guide*, *be.attitudes* (a 10 week Bible study), *Joseph: The Story of My Life* (a 10 week Bible study), *Blaze Your Trail* (a 10 week Bible study), and *The Move of a Lifetime* (moving Frank Lake Covenant Church)

Follow Kathy at kathyweckwerth.com or at bestlifeministries.com

More Books From

be.attitudes

A 10 week Bible study of Jesus' beatitudes found in Matthew chapter 5. When Jesus was teaching His disciples and followers on the mountainside that day, He delivered the attitudes of the heart that every Christ-follower should embrace and apply into their daily walk.

The Story of My Life: Joseph

A 10-week Bible study of Genesis chapters 37-50. Journey through the pages of Joseph's life and look at snapshots taken from the camera lens of the Bible, embrace the lessons learned throughout his trials from the pit, to the prison, to the palace.

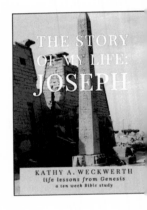

Blaze Your Trail

The Old West was a time where new territories were being explored, new ideas were being implemented, and new directions were being taken. In this 10 week Bible study, you will discover new territories in His plan, be motivated to embrace new ideas, and follow His divine new directions to live your Best Life.

Kathy A. Weckwerth

The Move of a Lifetime (Moving Frank Lake Covenant Church)

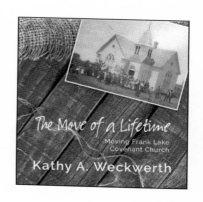

Built in 1900, and located in rural Murdock, MN, the church was set to be torn down when Kathy and her farmer-husband, Dean, purchased it. Follow the historical story of the founding of the church, the people who attended, the church's pastors, and the actual physical move to the Weckwerth's farm.

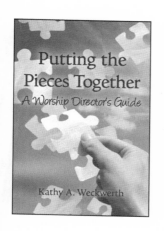

Putting the Pieces Together: A Worship Director's Guide

A how-to book that will help worship leaders, as well as pastors and church staff, put worship elements and effective strategy pieces into place to create powerful worship ministries.

Resources

Lesson 1

1. Ten Boom, C. (s.d.). BrainyQuoteÆ. Accessed January 2 2019 through https://www.brainyquote.com/quotes/corrie_ten_boom_381184

2. Swindoll, C. (2016). Watch Me Work. Accessed January 2 2019 through https://www.lightsource.com/ministry/insight-for-living/devotionals/todays-insight-from-chuck-swindoll/watch-me-work-todays-insight-july-27-2016-11757917.html

3. Henry, M. (s.d.). Commentary on the Whole Bible. Accessed January 2 2019 through https://www.biblestudytools.com/commentaries/matthew-henry-complete/

Lesson 2

1. Maxwell, J. (s.d.). AZ Quotes. Accessed January 2 2019 through https://www.azquotes.com/quote/615563

2. N. (s.d.). Dictionary by Merriam-Webster: America's most-trusted online dictionary. Accessed January 2 2019 through https://www.merriam-webster.com/

3. Alder, S. (s.d.). quotestoknow. Accessed January 2 2019 through https://www.quotes2know.com/Shannon-L-Alder-Quotes/101133

4. Disney, W. (s.d.). Brainy QuoteÆ. Accessed January 2, 2019 through https://www.brainyquote.com/quotes/walt_disney_130929

Lesson 3

1. Wiersbe, W. Be Amazed: Restoring an Attitude of Wonder and Worship. David C. Cook. 2012.

2. Swindoll, C. (1995). Attitude. Accessed January 2 2019 through https://officedynamics.com/attitude-by-charles-swindoll/

3. N. (s.d.). Dictionary by Merriam-Webster: America's most-trusted online dictionary. Accessed January 2 2019 through https://www.merriam-webster.com/

Lesson 4

1. Newton, J. (2013). Christian Quotes. Accessed January 2 2019 through https://www.christianquotes.info/top-quotes/18-amazing-quotes-about-gods-protection/#axzz5gfyS8m8R

2. N. (s.d.). Dictionary by Merriam-Webster: America's most-trusted online dictionary. Accessed January 2 2019 through https://www.merriam-webster.com/

3. Warren, R. (2013). The Purpose Driven Life. Accessed January 2 2019 through https://www.facebook.com/180199482041484/posts/fear-is-a-self-imposed-prison-that-will-keep-you-from-becoming-what-god-intends-/582875918440503/

4. Ten Boom, C. (s.d.). BrainyQuoteÆ. Accessed January 2 2019 through https://www.brainyquote.com/quotes/corrie_ten_boom_135203

5. Swindoll, C. (s.d.). Wise Old Sayings. Accessed January 2 2019 through http://www.wiseoldsayings.com/authors/charles-r.-swindoll-quotes/

Lesson 5

1. Graham, B. (s.d.). BrainyQuoteÆ. Accessed January 2 2019 through https://www.brainyquote.com/quotes/billy_graham_113622

2. Reagan, R. (1981). Inaugural Address. Accessed January 2 2019 through https://www.reaganfoundation.org/ronald-reagan/reagan-quotes-speeches/inaugural-address-5/

3. Maxwell, J. (s.d.). AZ Quotes. Accessed January 2 2019 through https://www.azquotes.com/quote/662105

Lesson 6

1. Lewis, C. S. (s.d.). C.S. Lewis Foundation. Accessed January 2 2019 through https://www.facebook.com/cslewisfound/posts/you-never-know-how-much-you-really-believe-anything-until-its-truth-or-falsehood/10156312209635169/

2. Kennedy, J. F. (s.d.). 10 Powerful Quotes from President John F. Kennedy. Accessed January 2 2019 through https://www.govloop.

com/10-powerful-quotes-from-president-john-f-kennedy/

3. Milton, J. (1600s). BrainyQuoteÆ. Accessed January 2 2019 through https://www.google.com/search

Lesson 7

1. Pascal, B. (s.d.). Inspirational Quotations. Accessed January 2 2019 through http://www.inspiration.rightattitudes.com/authors/blaise-pascal/

2. Spurgeon, C. (s.d.). Christian Quotes. Accessed January 2 2019 through https://www.christianquotes.info/images/charles-spurgeon-quote-doubt-kills-faith-delivers-personal-resurrection/#axzz5gfyS8m8R

3. Wiersbe. W.(1989).TheBibleExpositionCommentary. AccessedJanuary 2 2019 through https://books.google.com/books?isbn=1564760308

4. Ryle, J. C. (s.d.). Christian Quotes. Accessed January 2 2019 through https://www.christianquotes.info/quotes-by-author/j-c-ryle-quotes/?li stpage=4&instance=2#participants-list-2

5. Leaf, C. (2013). Switch On Your Brain. Accessed January 2 2019 through https://medium.com/baysidechurch/7-verses-about-the-power-of-your-thoughts-8a50b8e1910f

Lesson 8

1. Evans, T. (s.d.). Pinterest. Accessed January 2 2019 through https://www.pinterest.com/pin/49187820910912368/

2. Rogers, F. (s.d.). goodreads. Accessed January 2 2019 through https://www.goodreads.com/quotes/913279-as-human-beings-our-job-in-life-is-to-help

3. Drummond, H. (1900). Addresses by Henry Drummond. Accessed January 2 2019 through https://books.google.com/books?id=xFypBAA AQBAJ&pg=PT7&lpg=PT7&dq

4. Nyssa, G. (400s). Elders and the Word of Encouragement. Accessed January 2 2019 through https://slideplayer.com/slide/8457772/

Lesson 9

1. Campbell, D. (s.d.). Christian Quotes. Accessed January 2 2019 through https://www.christianquotes.info/quotes-by-author/duncan-campbell-quotes/#axzz5ghblBnbY

2. Ortberg, J. (2010). The Me I Want to Be. Accessed January 2 2019 through https://www.academia.edu/37982239/The_me_I_want_to_be_John_Ortberg

3. King, M. (s.d.). BrainyQuoteÆ. Accessed January 2 2019 through https://www.brainyquote.com/quotes/martin_luther_king_jr_390143

4. Reed, A. (1824). The Life of Washington. Accessed January 2 2019 through https://books.google.com/books?id=ry4TAQAAMAAJ&pg=PA111&lpg=PA111&dq=%22The+inhabitants+of+the+surrounding+country,+knowing+this+sad+state+of+the+army,+were+very+

Lesson 10

1. Ten Boom, C. (1984). goodreads. Accessed January 2 2019 through 9https://www.goodreads.com/quotes/1031360-i-know-that-the-experiences-of-our-lives-when-we

2. Carver, G. (s.d.). Smithsonian Natural World. Accessed January 2 2019 through https://www.smithsonianmag.com/photocontest/detail/natural-world/i-love-to-think-of-nature-as-an-unlimited-broadcasting-station-through-whic/